Ranchers, Homesteaders, and Traders

As the United States expanded westward, even popular songs urged settlers to make their way to newly opened territories like "the Kansas plains"—and, if necessary, to fight for the opportunity to build homesteads and cities there.

Ranchers, Homesteaders, and Traders

Frontiersmen of the South-Central States

Kieran Doherty

The Oliver Press, Inc.
Minneapolis

The Oliver Press, Inc.
Charlotte Square
5707 West 36th Street
Minneapolis, MN 55416-2510

Library of Congress Cataloging-in-Publication Data
Doherty, Kieran.
Ranchers, homesteaders, and traders: frontiersmen of the South-Central states / Kieran Doherty.
p.   cm. — (Shaping America ; 4)
Includes bibliographical references (p.) and index.
   Summary: Discusses the settlement of the south-central region of the United States through the lives of seven explorers and founders, including Daniel Boone in Kentucky and Stephen Austin and Sam Houston in Texas.
ISBN 1-881508-53-6
1. Pioneers—Southwest, Old—Biography—Juvenile Literature. 2. Frontier and pioneer life—Southwest, Old—Juvenile literature. 3. Southwest, Old—Biography—Juvenile literature. 4. Southwest, Old—History—Juvenile literature. [1. Pioneers. 2. Frontier and pioneer life—Southwest, Old. 3. Southwest, Old—history.] I. Title. II. Series.
F396.D64 2000
976'.009'9—dc21
[B]   00-052864
                                               CIP
                                               AC
ISBN 1-881508-53-6
Printed in the United States of America
07 06 05 04 03 02 01   8 7 6 5 4 3 2 1

Contents

6

Introduction

The story of the vast territory of America has been shaped by one wave of immigrants after another. The very first settlers were prehistoric men and women who came from Asia more than 30,000 years ago. They crossed the Bering Strait from Siberia to western Alaska over the Bering Land Bridge, a dry causeway that then joined North America and Asia. Over thousands of years, these immigrants spread south to the tip of South America and east across all of present-day Canada and the United States. During this time, they adapted to their surroundings and eventually evolved to become the various peoples we know as Native Americans.

In the eastern and central parts of what is now the United States lived a group of Native American cultures known as the mound builders. Over a period of several thousand years, these peoples constructed large earthen mounds for a variety of purposes. Starting around 500 B.C., the Adena people, who lived in the Ohio River valley, built large burial mounds for important members of the tribe. About 400 years later, the people of the Hopewell civilization,

This map shows the gradual expansion of the United States as explorers, traders, and settlers pressed relentlessly westward in search of open lands and new opportunities.

which was centered in the same region, also built burial mounds in their villages. Mound building reached its peak in the Mississippian culture, which originated in the lower Mississippi valley around A.D. 700 and eventually spread throughout most of the eastern half of North America, reaching as far west as Oklahoma. Mississippian mounds usually served as bases or foundations for public buildings, including temples. These buildings were often arranged around an open plaza and served as community centers.

For centuries, the mound builders and other Native American civilizations lived undisturbed in North America, never dreaming that different societies were developing in distant lands across the oceans. Then suddenly, late in the 1400s, they were forced to become aware of these other cultures when European explorers arrived in the New World of the Americas. Within a century, a second great wave of immigrants began pouring into North and South America.

During the 1500s, the Spanish built frontier outposts along the northern edge of their New World empire, which was centered in Mexico. At the same time, the French established their own frontier settlements in what is now eastern Canada. Spurred on by the riches of the fur trade, French explorers, adventurers, trappers, and traders were soon building military outposts around the Great Lakes, along the Mississippi River, and on the shores of the Gulf of Mexico. By the time the English appeared on the American scene in 1585, attempting to found a colony at Roanoke Island off the coast of what is now North Carolina, the Spanish and French had firmly established their frontier empires in North America. Soon, however, English settlements were springing up from the northern border of Florida all the way along the Atlantic coast to what is now the Canadian border.

By this time, only a few mound-builder settlements were active in the south-central region of the continent. In present-day Mississippi, the Natchez people were still building temple and burial mounds in their villages near the Mississippi River. As Europeans established settlements in the region during the 1700s, the Natchez, the last of the great mound-building cultures, gradually disappeared. But the legacy of the mound builders lived on among their descendants, which included the Cherokee, Creek, Choctaw, and Chickasaw tribes.

This book tells the story of the European settlement of the lands on which these and other Native American groups lived—now the south-central states of the United States. It recounts the lives and exploits of seven men who explored and tamed the wild territory that was once America's western frontier. In the process, they made it possible for countless thousands of other immigrants to follow in their footsteps and develop these areas as we know them today.

Some of the pioneers included in this book are French explorers and traders who helped to expand France's foothold in North America. Henry de Tonty was an adventurer who served as second-in-command to the great French explorer Robert de La Salle.

Among the first Europeans to travel all the way down the Mississippi River from the Great Lakes to the Gulf of Mexico, Tonty was also the founder of the first European settlement in what is now Arkansas. Auguste Chouteau, meanwhile, was a fur trader who supervised the founding of the city of St. Louis, Missouri, while he was still a teenager and saw the city grow into a major center of settlement and trade.

Other pioneers were American-born descendants of some of the earliest English settlers along the Atlantic coast. Daniel Boone, the famous backwoodsman and hunter, led settlers through the Cumberland Gap into Kentucky and founded several settlements there. John Sevier, a Revolutionary War hero, was one of the first settlers in the Watauga

Thousands of easterners packed their families and belongings into covered wagons and set off toward the ever-changing western frontier.

region of Tennessee and became that state's first governor. Stephen Austin drew American settlers into his colony in what was then part of Mexico, gaining fame as the Father of Texas. And Samuel Houston, though not the founder of a settlement, was one of the main figures responsible for Texas becoming part of the United States.

Most unusual is the story of Eli Thayer, who never even set foot in the state he helped to settle. In an attempt to keep Kansas from entering the Union as a slave state during the 1850s, Thayer helped several thousand antislavery homesteaders make their way to the Kansas frontier. These settlers ultimately founded a number of cities, and their passionate struggle against slavery ensured that Kansas became a free state.

All of these frontiersmen had different motives for their exploits. Some, including Henry de Tonty and Auguste Chouteau, were driven by their ambition for worldly fame and wealth. Others, such as Stephen Austin, John Sevier, and Daniel Boone, hungered for new land where they could settle and find success—a hunger felt by thousands of other immigrants who left the settlements along the Atlantic coast and moved west. Sam Houston and Eli Thayer, on the other hand, were more compelled by the desire for justice than the search for land. But whatever their motivations, these pioneers of the south-central states lived lives of courage and dedication that helped to shape the United States as we know it.

Chapter One

Henry de Tonty
and the
First Settlement in Arkansas

On July 14, 1678, a small ship named the *Saint Honoré* left the port of La Rochelle on the coast of France. On board the 200-ton vessel were the ship's crew and 30 adventurers recruited for a trading and exploring venture in the vast area of North America then known as New France.

The little ship—only about 120 feet long—soon made its way into the trackless expanse of the Atlantic Ocean. The ocean crossing was difficult, marred by terrible storms common in the Atlantic during the summer hurricane season. Finally, on August 20, after five weeks at sea, the *Saint Honoré* entered the mouth of the St. Lawrence River.

For the next three weeks, the vessel made its slow way up the St. Lawrence. On September 15, the *Saint Honoré* dropped anchor in the harbor of

Few pictures exist of Henry de Tonty (1649?-1704), who spent much of his career in the shadow of Robert de La Salle— the great explorer whom he served as second-in-command. In this drawing of La Salle's party reaching the mouth of the Mississippi River, the man raising the sword is La Salle and the man standing to the right with his arms crossed is probably Tonty.

Quebec, the capital city of New France. The first man off the ship was probably René Robert Cavelier, sieur de La Salle, a dashing adventurer already famous for his exploits in the lands that the French had claimed in the New World. La Salle was the leader of this latest expedition to discover new lands and to strengthen the French presence in North America.

At La Salle's side (or perhaps slightly behind him) as he strode ashore would have been Henry de Tonty, his second-in-command. Tonty of the Iron Hand, as he was known, was a brave veteran of military battles that had won him limited fame in France. Now Tonty stood on the threshold of a new career as an explorer, adventurer, and trader—and ultimately as the founder of the first European settlement in the land we know today as Arkansas.

The details of Tonty's earliest years have been lost in the shadows of the past. Henry de Tonty (sometimes spelled Tonti) was born in either 1649 or 1650. He was the first son—and perhaps the first child—of Lorenzo de Tonty, a famous banker, and Lorenzo's wife, Isabelle. The place of Henry's birth is uncertain, though many scholars believe it was the ancient fortress city of Gaeta in Italy, where his father served as governor.

Although Italian by birth, Lorenzo de Tonty eventually became an influential man in the court of the French king, Louis XIV. Young Henry spent his boyhood in Paris and, as the son of one of the leaders at court, he almost certainly attended one of the city's Roman Catholic schools.

In 1653, Lorenzo de Tonty proposed a remarkable plan to strengthen the French government's finances. People would contribute small sums of money to a fund that paid them interest. As investors died off, payments to the surviving contributors would increase. When no investors remained, the French government would receive the leftover money. The plan was put into action, but it failed, largely because the French were suspicious of the foreign-born Tonty. Displeased, King Louis XIV imprisoned him in the Bastille until 1677. Tonty was a broken man, but his name lived on: the type of insurance scheme he created became known as a "tontine."

In 1668, when Henry de Tonty was about 18 years of age, he entered the French army and later became a sea-going soldier. During the next several years, he fought against the Spanish, who were warring with France for control of the Mediterranean Sea. In one of these battles, his right hand was terribly maimed by a grenade. According to legend, Tonty, unwilling to wait for a doctor, used his own sword to hack off his wounded hand. During this same battle, he was captured by the enemy.

After being released in a prisoner exchange, Tonty was granted a small pension by the king in honor of his services. Disabled by the loss of his hand, he might have been expected to stay ashore. Instead, he immediately volunteered to go to sea again, serving honorably until the war between Spain and France ended in 1678.

At the end of the war, Tonty was fitted with a metal hand, probably made of brass. We don't know for sure what this hand was like; it may have been no more than a hook. It seems, however, that it was capable of movement. Tonty's artificial hand, which he covered with a glove, enabled him to perform many tasks that required two hands. He became so skillful in its use that the loss of his real hand soon was little more than a nuisance.

Around this time, events were unfolding that would soon enable Tonty to find both work and fame far from his home in France. With the European wars at an end, at least for a time, France was able to turn its attention to the vast and mostly unexplored lands of the New World. King Louis and his advisors

Tonty used his "iron hand" with great effect on rebellious men or on anyone who displeased him, employing it as a kind of club to beat them into submission. The Indians of New France often referred to him as *Bras-de-fer*, meaning "Iron Arm," or *Bras-coupé*, "Cut-off Arm."

knew that the English were rapidly establishing settlements along the eastern coast of North America and that the Spanish were firmly entrenched in the lands to the southwest. The French had established some settlements in what is now Canada and had built Fort Niagara near present-day Buffalo, New York. They had also built and later abandoned forts in Maine and Vermont. Now the time had come for France to explore and exploit the rest of North America.

At this time, too, the explorer Robert de La Salle returned to France from the New World with plans to establish a series of trading posts in the Mississippi River valley. The king was intrigued by his proposal, especially when La Salle announced

René Robert Cavelier, sieur de La Salle (1643-1687) was the son of a rich French merchant. As a boy, he began training to become a Jesuit priest, but he left the religious life at the age of 23 to sail for Montreal, Canada, and seek his fortune. Except for periodic visits to France, La Salle spent the rest of his life exploring North America.

that he would finance the scheme himself, using money raised from investors.

Tonty soon learned of La Salle's plans for exploration and settlement in the New World. Desperately in need of employment, the one-handed soldier let several influential friends know of his desire to join La Salle's expedition. They interceded with the famed explorer on Tonty's behalf. Eager to stay in favor with the powerful members of the court, La Salle made Tonty his second-in-command, a decision he would never have cause to regret. Tonty soon became La Salle's most loyal follower and a tireless worker for his goals in the New World.

After the two men met in Paris, La Salle's plans were quickly set in motion and the *Saint Honoré* departed for the New World. In addition to its crew and passengers, it carried the supplies needed to establish outposts in the wilderness. Its cargo also included masts, anchors, and rigging to be used in constructing ships that the explorers could sail down the Mississippi in search of likely sites for forts or trading posts.

Late in 1678, Tonty, La Salle, and their party left Quebec and sailed down the St. Lawrence River to Fort Frontenac, at the site of the present-day city of Kingston on the shores of Lake Ontario. From Frontenac, Tonty and about 30 men made their way southwest to the Niagara River, which connects Lake Ontario and Lake Erie. There, Tonty said, they intended "to look for a suitable place above the falls where a boat might be built." After finding a likely spot, Tonty and his men built the *Griffon*, a small

"At that time the late M. Cavelier de La Salle came to court, a man of great intelligence and merit, who sought to obtain leave from the court to explore the Gulf of Mexico by traversing the countries of North America. . . . The late Monseigneur the Prince of Conti, who was acquainted with [La Salle] . . . sent me to ask him to be allowed to accompany him in his long journeys, to which he very willingly assented."
—Henry de Tonty

"M. de Tonty has always employed so honest a manner towards me, that I cannot overstate my joy in having him with me. . . . He has surpassed my highest hopes. . . . His honesty and intrinsic worth are well enough known to you, but perhaps you would not have believed him capable of doing things for which a strong constitution, a knowledge of country, and the free use of two arms seem absolutely necessary."
—Robert de La Salle

The Griffon *was named for a mythological beast that was half lion and half eagle. As the boat was being built, La Salle bragged that he would "make the* Griffon *fly above the crows." Disproving his prideful boast, the vessel sank two years later.*

two-masted vessel designed to transport them through the Great Lakes.

When the boat was finished, Tonty and a small band of explorers made their way in canoes to the extreme western end of Lake Erie. There, Tonty and his men met the *Griffon*, which had crossed Lake Erie under the command of La Salle. From this point, the entire group sailed through the series of waterways (along the eastern coast of what is now the state of Michigan) that link Lake Erie and Lake

Huron—the Detroit River, Lake St. Clair, and the St. Clair River. They then crossed Lake Huron to French-held Fort Michilimackinac, located on the southern side of the Straits of Mackinac between Lakes Huron and Michigan.

At the fort, Tonty and La Salle separated. La Salle, with a group of men, traveled southwest on Lake Michigan to the site of what is now Green Bay, Wisconsin, to trade with the Indians for furs. He then sent the *Griffon*, loaded with a small fortune in

As this map demonstrates, the rivers and lakes of what is now southeastern Canada and the northeastern United States provided natural highways for French and British explorers and traders as they traveled inland in the seventeenth and eighteenth centuries. The general route of Tonty and his men to Fort Michilimackinac is marked.

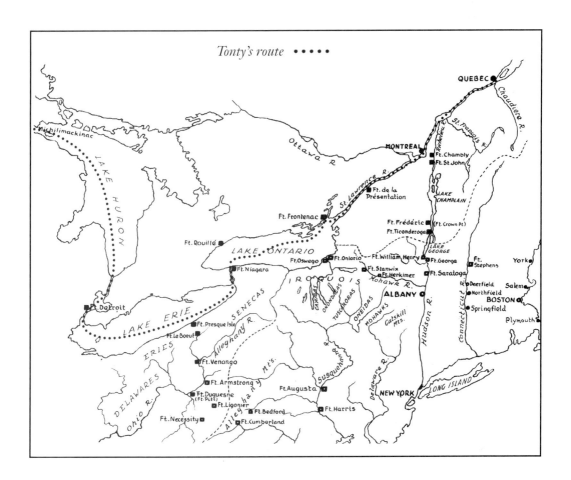

La Salle's men load precious furs into a small boat that will take them to the Griffon *(anchored offshore).*

pelts, through the Great Lakes back to Fort Niagara, while he proceeded down Lake Michigan to the mouth of the St. Joseph River, on the lake's eastern shore. Tonty, meanwhile, made his own way with a handful of followers by canoe south along the eastern coast of Lake Michigan until he rejoined La Salle at the St. Joseph River.

During the next several months, the two men and their followers left the Great Lakes region to explore what is now the state of Illinois. Traveling by river and carrying their canoes from one river to the next, they finally reached the Illinois River and descended it for about 250 miles. By January 3, 1680, when they arrived at a spot near the site of present-day Peoria, Illinois, Tonty and La Salle knew they would have to build shelter against the winter weather. They quickly erected a fort on the banks of the river. Some idea of the hardships they faced can be gained from the fort's name, Crevecoeur, which means "heartbreak" in French.

In late March, La Salle and some of his men set out on foot to try to learn what had become of the *Griffon*, the ship that the explorer had earlier sent to Fort Niagara with a load of furs. He left Tonty in command of Fort Crevecoeur, with about two dozen men. Eventually La Salle would learn that the *Griffon* had been sunk during a storm on Lake Michigan, its crew and its valuable cargo lost.

Not long after La Salle's departure, while Tonty was briefly away from the fort, almost all his men deserted. "They took away everything that was finest and most valuable," the French explorer later wrote, "and left me with two [Franciscan friars] and five Frenchmen, newly arrived from France, stripped of everything and at the mercy of the savages."

Although he could have fled from Fort Crevecoeur—and would probably have been justified in leaving—Tonty chose to stay. He sent a report to La Salle informing him that he was virtually alone in the wilderness. Tonty and the handful of men with him managed to survive the summer as they waited for their commander to return.

In the autumn of 1680, a large party of warlike Iroquois entered the lands of the Illinois Indians, with whom the French had established good relations.

Tonty's deserting men burned Fort Crevecoeur, leaving behind only a plank of wood carved with a message: "We are all savages."

A French drawing of a tattooed Iroquois Indian holding a snake and smoking a peace pipe, from about 1701. The Iroquois, a confederacy of five tribes (the Mohawk, Oneida, Onondaga, Cayuga, and Seneca), were one of the most politically organized and militarily strong Native American groups in North America. Allying themselves with the British, they fiercely opposed the French presence in their region.

"When I had come up to them, these wretches [the Iroquois] seized me, took the necklace from my hand, and one of them, reaching through the crowd, plunged a knife into my breast, wounding a rib near the heart."
—Henry de Tonty

The Illinois were alarmed by this invasion, and Tonty was quickly drafted to serve as a peacemaker. Taking gifts of wampum—the beads used as money by many Native Americans—he entered the Iroquois camp, where he was attacked and seriously wounded.

Tonty survived the attack, but he was held prisoner by the Iroquois. He tried to convince his captors that it would be foolhardy to wage war with the Illinois, who were under the protection of La Salle and the French king. Finally, he managed to escape.

When it became obvious that the Illinois and the Iroquois were going to fight, Tonty and his followers fled Fort Crevecoeur. For about a month, he and the others traveled north, first by canoe and later on foot, as they struggled to reach the French settlements. Sometime in late 1680, Tonty and his men—except for one Franciscan priest killed by Indians when he wandered away from the main party—reached Green Bay and safety.

The next several years were busy ones for Tonty. In mid-1681, after he rejoined La Salle at Michilimackinac, the two adventurers set out to

During their flight from Fort Crevecoeur, Tonty and his men faced many hardships. "During this time," Tonty later recalled, "we lived on nothing but wild garlic, which we were obliged to grub up under the snow."

During Tonty's time, Fort Michilimackinac was one of the most crucial French military outposts and trading headquarters. Although its importance declined after the city of Detroit was founded in 1701, the fort still stands today.

explore the Mississippi River, reaching the mouth of the river and the Gulf of Mexico on April 7, 1682. This journey of exploration is, perhaps, La Salle's greatest claim to fame. Not only did it expand the French presence in North America, but it also provided a route to the ocean by which furs and other goods could easily be transported to Europe.

On the way back to the Illinois lands, Tonty and La Salle built Fort St. Louis on a natural formation called Starved Rock, overlooking the Illinois River. Then, in the autumn of 1683, La Salle sailed off to France to report to the king on his explorations. He left Tonty behind to watch over his interests in the New World.

Tonty spent most of the next three years in Green Bay and other French settlements in the north. Back in France, La Salle secured government support for his plans to colonize Louisiana, as he had named the vast New World territory he had discovered. His commission from the king gave him the right to claim for France all the land stretching south from the Illinois country to the Gulf of Mexico and west from the Mississippi River to the Spanish territories. In 1684, he assembled a flotilla of ships and set sail from France, bound for the Gulf of Mexico. This second La Salle expedition would eventually end in failure.

Tonty knew of La Salle's commission from the king, but by early 1686, he had heard no news about the fate of the expedition. He decided that he would head down the Mississippi River in search of the man who was both his friend and his commander. On

In early 1685, La Salle and his men—unable to find the mouth of the Mississippi River—had been shipwrecked on the Gulf Coast of Texas, where they built a fort and struggled to survive. It soon became plain that they would not be rescued, and in January 1687 La Salle led an overland expedition to try to reach Tonty in Illinois. On March 19, somewhere in eastern Texas, La Salle was murdered by his disenchanted followers. The men who killed La Salle were then put to death by other members of the party. This illustration shows the tragic aftermath of the La Salle expedition.

February 13, 1686, Tonty set out with 25 Frenchmen, 5 Illinois Indians, and 4 Shawnee Indians. The party made good time, reaching the Gulf of Mexico on April 9, but found no sign of La Salle. Still determined to find the explorer, Tonty dispatched canoes to search the Gulf Coast for about 100 miles to the east and west of the mouth of the Mississippi.

When these searches proved futile, Tonty proposed returning to Canada by following the coast east, around the south end of Florida, and then north all the way to New York, proceeding overland from there to Montreal. In that way, he told his men, "we might discover some fine country and might even take some prize on our way." Such a journey would have guaranteed Tonty's fame as an explorer. Unfortunately for his reputation, however, his men were against the plan, so it was abandoned.

On the journey back up the Mississippi, Tonty took the time to establish a trading settlement at the spot where the Arkansas and Mississippi Rivers meet. Under his direction, a small house surrounded by a palisade (a defensive wall) was constructed. This fort—the first permanent European settlement in the lower Mississippi valley—was intended to serve as a link between the French settlements in Louisiana and those in Canada. It would also be a means of maintaining good relations with Native Americans of the region.

This 1718 map shows French Louisiana extending across most of what is now the eastern and central United States. Much of the land is identified by the names of the Native Americans who lived there, and the French settlements are concentrated near the Gulf of Mexico or the Great Lakes.

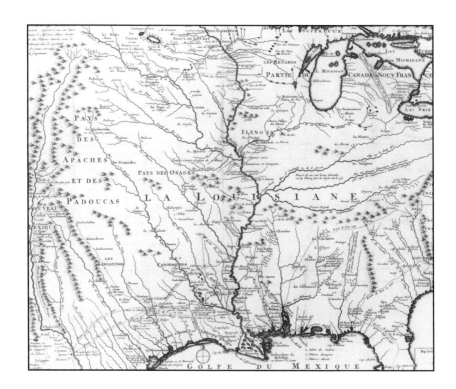

Arkansas before Tonty

The arrival of Europeans disrupted the life that Native Americans had lived for generations. This drawing shows Indians setting fire to their village and fleeing as de Soto approaches.

Almost 3,000 years before the first Europeans saw the land that is now Arkansas, the region was home to the bluff dwellers, Native Americans who lived mostly in the northwestern part of the state. Later inhabitants of the Arkansas region were members of the mound-builder civilization, prehistoric people who created earthen mounds that were used as burial sites or temple platforms.

In 1541, Hernando de Soto and his men became the first Europeans to visit Arkansas when they traveled across the state in search of treasure. At that time, the region was home to three major Native American tribes, the Osage, Caddo, and Quapaw (or Arkansas) Indians. These Indian people are believed to be descendants of the ancient mound builders.

Following de Soto's visit, no Europeans are known to have visited Arkansas until 1673. In that year, a group of French explorers led by Louis Joliet and Father Jacques Marquette traveled down the Mississippi River as far as the Arkansas River. About 10 years later, Robert de La Salle journeyed down the Mississippi to its end at the Gulf of Mexico. He claimed the lands on the west bank of the river, including the area that would become Arkansas, for France.

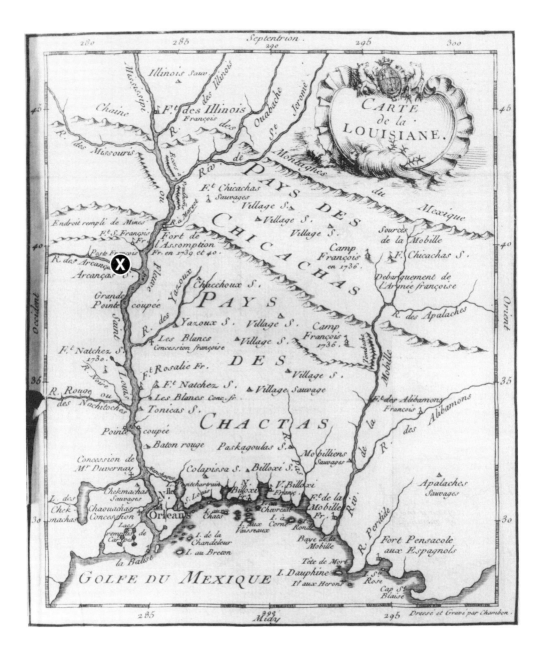

This map shows the strategic location of Tonty's fort (labeled "Poste François") near the meeting of the Arkansas and Mississippi Rivers.

Although Tonty's fort began as little more than an outpost, it was on its way to becoming an important trading center in French Louisiana during the late seventeenth century. The French government's hopes that settlers would pour into the region were not realized, however, and during the early years of the eighteenth century, the settlement was abandoned. But its story was not yet ended.

In 1720, a flamboyant financier named John Law promoted the lands of what we now know as Louisiana and Arkansas as ideal places for settlement. He convinced more than 700 German men, women, and children to establish a community near the site of Tonty's original fort. Although the settlers relocated when Law's financial schemes collapsed, the settlement—called Arkansas Post—endured. In 1783, it was the site of the Colbert Incident, the only Revolutionary War battle to occur in Arkansas. Then, after the War of 1812, land-hungry American settlers rapidly populated the area, and Arkansas Post became the capital of the Arkansas Territory. The capital was moved to Little Rock in 1821, but Arkansas Post remained an important trading center and steamboat stop, and it was the site of a battle during the Civil War.

After Tonty established the original settlement in Arkansas in 1686, he did not spend much time there. In September 1689, when he learned of La Salle's death, he set out to find survivors of the tragic expedition, but had no luck. For the next 10 years, Tonty remained in the Illinois lands and was successful in bringing settlers, supplies, trade goods,

Scotsman John Law (1671-1729) was a banker and financier who attracted the attention of King Louis XIV by proposing a new government credit system and the rapid exploitation of North America as a way to make money. Appointed controller-general of French finance in 1720, he was made responsible for the settlement of the Mississippi valley. He urged the printing of vast amounts of paper money so that people could buy shares in public companies responsible for the region's settlement. While Law's plan did inspire the establishment of several colonies, including Arkansas Post, his scheme soon led to inflation and a huge financial crash. Disgraced, Law fled to Vienna, where he died.

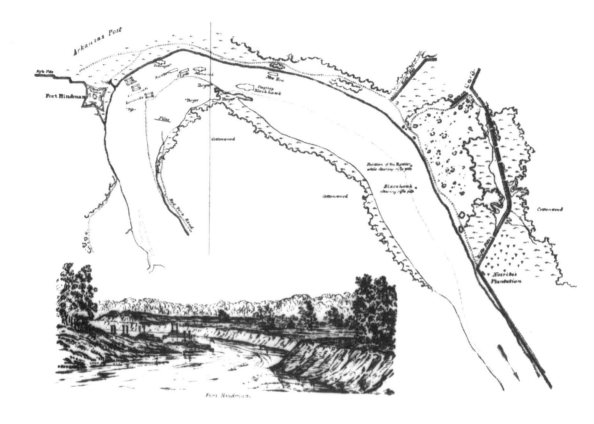

Fort Hindman.

During the Civil War, Confederate troops tried to maintain control of the strategic spot where the Arkansas and Mississippi Rivers meet. They built a large earthen fortification called Fort Hindman in 1862 to protect the area near Arkansas Post. In January 1863, however, Union troops attacked and destroyed the fort and the adjacent town. This map was made soon after the Union gained control of the area.

and Catholic missionaries into the region from Canada.

In 1700, Tonty heard about the founding of New Orleans by Pierre le Moyne d'Iberville. He allied himself with Iberville and spent about four years in what is now the state of Louisiana, exploring the wilderness and establishing peaceful relations with the Indians. In 1704, while in Mobile, Alabama, Tonty died, apparently of yellow fever.

Today, Henry de Tonty's exploits remain largely unknown. A modest man, Tonty never boasted of his own accomplishments as explorers such as La Salle often did. Though he is usually considered little more than a faithful lieutenant to the much more famous La Salle, Tonty was himself a great explorer and settler and deserves recognition as the founder of the first settlement in what is now the state of Arkansas.

Arkansas after Tonty

After the ultimate failure of John Law's Mississippi Scheme, settlement of Arkansas by France slowed dramatically. In 1762, the French ceded Arkansas and their other possessions west of the Mississippi River to Spain in exchange for Spain's help during the French and Indian War.

The Spanish hoped to attract settlers to the region, especially people from the newly established United States, but they were no more successful than the French had been. When Spain ceded the region back to France in 1800, the total population of what is now Arkansas included fewer than 1,000 Europeans.

Three years later, the Louisiana Purchase made Arkansas—along with the rest of the area between the Mississippi River and the Rocky Mountains—part of the growing United States. During the next two decades, Arkansas was part of what was first known as the Louisiana District, then as the Louisiana Territory, and finally as the Missouri Territory. Settlers began to arrive, establishing farms on the rich soil along the Mississippi River. In 1819, the region was recognized as the Arkansas Territory, a step that would make it possible for Arkansas to become a state.

Until this time, settlement of the region had been relatively slow, largely due to a government decision to move some Cherokee and Choctaw Indians to Arkansas from their homes in Tennessee. Following the removal of those Native American groups to areas farther west in 1820, the pace of settlement increased dramatically, and by 1825, Arkansas had 50,000 white residents. Spurred by the booming cotton industry, the population continued to grow, and on June 15, 1836, Arkansas became the 25th state to join the Union.

Chapter Two

Auguste Chouteau
and
St. Louis, Missouri

O n a mid-February day in 1764, a teenaged boy stood atop a limestone bluff just a few miles south of the spot where the Missouri River joins the Mississippi River. Looking down on the Mississippi, Auguste Chouteau could see the great river rolling its way south toward the Gulf of Mexico. Gazing off to the west, he saw a seemingly endless expanse of trees and grassland. Though there was no way he could have known it at the time, 14-year-old Auguste was about to begin a lifelong adventure that would make him the master of virtually all he saw and bring him fame as one of the shapers of America.

Auguste Chouteau was born in New Orleans in early September 1749. Although we don't know his exact birthday, we do know that he was baptized in

The leading member of what became known as "The First Family of St. Louis," Auguste Chouteau (1749-1829) not only helped to initiate a booming fur trade in Missouri, but he also planned the city of St. Louis and became one of its most influential citizens.

Pierre de Laclède Liguest (1729-1778) was born in France to a prominent family whose members included attorneys, scholars, and politicians. Confident and well educated, Laclède arrived in New Orleans in 1755 and quickly established himself as a successful businessman. Not long after his arrival, he met Marie Thérèse Bourgeois Chouteau (1733-1814), a resourceful young woman struggling to support herself and her six-year-old son.

the Cathedral of St. Louis on September 7 of that year, so he was probably born a few days earlier. His father, René, was an innkeeper who had emigrated from France to America sometime in the 1740s. His mother, Marie Thérèse Bourgeois, had been born in the French territory of Louisiana.

About a year after Auguste's birth, his father abandoned his mother, leaving Marie Thérèse and her infant son to fend for themselves. Soon, however, she met Pierre de Laclède Liguest, a man who was to play an important role in young Auguste's life and in the settlement of Missouri. By 1757, Marie Thérèse and Pierre were living together, married in all but name. Their union was frowned upon by the Roman Catholic Church, but it was to last for the rest of their lives, even withstanding a challenge when Marie Thérèse's lawful husband reappeared years later.

Marie Thérèse and Pierre had four children: Jean Pierre, born in 1758; Marie Pelagie, born in 1760; Marie Louise, born in 1762; and Victoire, born in 1764. Since neither the Catholic Church nor the New Orleans government recognized separation or divorce, Marie Thérèse was forced to continue using the Chouteau name, and each of the children was, in turn, christened with that name.

During his boyhood years, Auguste Chouteau appears to have been very close to Pierre de Laclède. Though we don't know for sure, Laclède probably saw to it that Auguste received a good education in one of the Catholic schools in New Orleans. By the time Auguste was in his teens, he was employed as a clerk in his stepfather's thriving trading business.

In August 1763, Auguste joined Laclède on a journey up the Mississippi River to what was then known as the Illinois Country. Here his stepfather planned to establish a trading post. To young Auguste, the journey must have been a mixture of excitement and boredom as the barges filled with merchandise made their slow way north against the river current. Day after day, burly barge men poled the heavy vessels along the winding river or raised small sails to take advantage of any favorable winds that blew. Even with the wind's help, the heavily loaded barges averaged only about 10 miles per day.

In early November, after a 700-mile journey, the expedition finally arrived in the tiny village of Ste. Genevieve, on the river's west bank. Leaving his trade goods in storage at nearby Fort Chartres, Laclède, accompanied by Auguste, set out to find a suitable location for his planned trading post. For several weeks, they searched the lands along the west bank of the river before Laclède finally decided on a spot not far from the place where the Missouri River joined the Mississippi.

The location appeared ideal. It was high on a bluff, protected from seasonal flooding, but with easy access to the Mississippi, Missouri, and Illinois Rivers. After he returned to Fort Chartres, Laclède bragged that the spot he chose would someday be the site of "one of the finest cities in America."

Ste. Genevieve, the first permanent settlement in Missouri, was about 50 miles south of the site Laclède chose for his new city.

Missouri before Chouteau

Long before Europeans saw the lands we know today as Missouri, the region was home to several Native American groups. Among the earliest were members of the mound-builder culture, who were later supplanted by a number of regional tribes, including the Missouri and the Osage.

The Missouri lived along the Missouri River in permanent villages. During most of the year, their homes were lodges made of earth, and they subsisted largely on maize (corn), beans, and squash that they cultivated. During hunting season, the Missouri would travel to the plains, where they lived in portable teepees while hunting bison. The other major tribe in the area, the Osage, had its traditional homeland in western Missouri near the Osage River. The Osage also lived by hunting and farming.

The rich lands inhabited by these Native Americans were untouched by Europeans until 1673, when they were first explored by the Jesuit priest Father Jacques Marquette and the fur trader Louis Joliet. The region that is now Missouri was claimed for France in 1682 by the explorer and adventurer Robert de La Salle, becoming part of the territory known as Louisiana. Following the discovery of rich lead deposits nearby, a small settlement was founded at Ste. Genevieve in about 1735. Larger settlements soon followed as Europeans realized the importance of Missouri as a source of furs.

Marquette and Joliet canoed down the Mississippi River from Wisconsin to southern Missouri.

Early the next spring, Auguste—by that time Laclède's trusted second-in-command, despite his youth—was sent north to begin construction of the new settlement. He took with him 30 laborers and the supplies needed for clearing the land and constructing buildings. On February 14, 1764, they reached the spot Laclède had chosen. The next day, the men set to work.

Construction under Auguste's direction went smoothly. When Laclède arrived at the new settlement in early April, he found his young stepson in command of a tiny community that already included several cabins and a storage shed for trade goods.

Workmen under Chouteau's direction began work on the new city as soon as the Mississippi had thawed enough for them to travel upriver with tools and supplies.

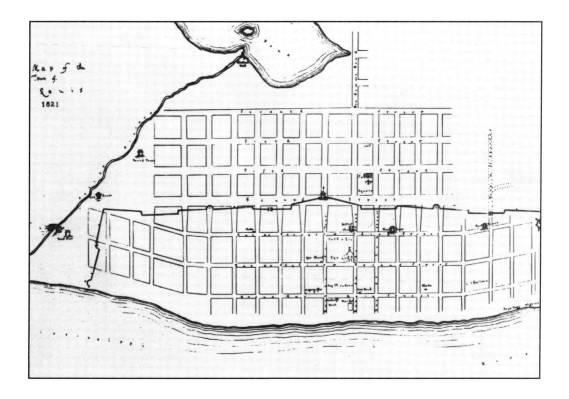

During his visit, Laclède told Auguste to see to it that the town was laid out in a grid pattern, like the city of New Orleans. The trader's plans called for three streets running parallel to the Mississippi River, intersected by a series of short cross streets, with a public plaza built on the waterfront. At that time, Laclède named the city St. Louis, in honor of the patron saint of Louis XV, the reigning king of France.

Even as the tiny settlement on the banks of the river was taking shape, events were occurring that would guarantee its success. France had given New Orleans and the French lands west of the Mississippi River to Spain, its ally in the French and Indian War,

By 1821, the original three streets parallel to the river had become seven, but St. Louis still retained the grid pattern developed by Laclède and Chouteau.

in the 1762 Treaty of Fontainbleu. The war had ended in 1763, with the English defeating the French and winning control of all lands east of the Mississippi River. Faced with the certainty that they would soon be under the rule of their British enemies, many French-speaking residents of the Louisiana territory fled to New Orleans. Others moved west, across the river to St. Louis. Young Auguste Chouteau made these immigrants welcome and offered them as much assistance as he could, knowing that they would only help to make the settlement stronger.

The young founder's plans to create a great city in the wilderness were threatened in 1764 when a large group of Missouri Indian warriors and their families arrived in St. Louis and announced that they intended to settle there. Although the Native Americans were not warlike, many of the white settlers who had moved across the river to live in the town quickly decamped and went back to their homes in British territory. Chouteau knew enough to realize that he did not have the experience to deal with this threat to the success of his settlement. He immediately sent for Laclède, who was then living in Fort Chartres.

Laclède responded to his stepson's call for help and rushed to St. Louis, where he negotiated with the leaders of the Missouri Indian group. Chouteau must have watched intently as his stepfather used a mixture of threats and promises of gifts to convince the Native Americans to leave. Later in his life, Chouteau would use these same techniques often in his dealings with other Indians.

Once the Missouri Indians were persuaded to settle in some other location, St. Louis once again began thriving. Chouteau oversaw the construction of the trading post, a large stone building not far from the waterfront. Soon after that building was completed in September 1764, Auguste's mother and his brother and sisters arrived in the rapidly growing community. They lived in Laclède's trading post until 1768, when a large house was completed for them.

During this period, St. Louis grew steadily as settlers streamed in, hoping to take advantage of the city's obviously favorable location as a trading center. The stream became something like a flood in late 1765, after the British actually arrived to take possession of the lands east of the Mississippi. At that time, many of the residents of Fort Chartres who had been reluctant to leave their homes quickly moved to St. Louis. Some of those fleeing British rule actually dismantled their homes and hauled lumber, door frames, windows, and anything else they could carry to the rapidly growing town on the west bank of the Mississippi.

It was not long before St. Louis became the most important fur-trading center in the upper Mississippi River valley. Indians came from throughout the region to trade precious beaver pelts and other furs to enterprising businessmen like Laclède. The furs were then shipped downriver to New Orleans. Just three years after the first cabin had been built in the settlement, St. Louis was not just the main commercial center on the northern reaches of the Mississippi, but it also served as the seat of

By 1767, St. Louis was a thriving small town with more than 75 dwellings scattered along the river's edge. Most of these were small cabins with walls made of posts driven into the ground. A few, however, were more elaborate homes, such as the stone dwelling that Laclède built for Marie Thérèse and their children. This was a large building, measuring about 50 by 35 feet, with a shingled roof and wooden floors and ceilings. Since St. Louis had no separate commercial district in its early days, Laclède—like other merchants and traders—ran his business from home.

St. Louis was a convenient spot for Native American and French trappers—like those shown here—to do business with traders, who could easily transport the furs down the Mississippi to New Orleans, and from there overseas.

government for the French authorities in Upper Louisiana. With a population that numbered more than 300, it was a success. Auguste Chouteau, still a teenager, could look over the city he had founded for his stepfather and feel justifiable pride.

In 1767, the Spanish suddenly seized control of St. Louis in accordance with the treaty with France that had promised them control of New Orleans and the lands west of the Mississippi. Although some of the city's French residents were apprehensive about the change, the transfer of power went smoothly.

The arrival of Spanish authorities sent by King Carlos III actually proved beneficial to Laclède and Chouteau, who were more than willing to cooperate with the new rulers. One of the first official acts of the Spanish government was to establish a system for the licensing of all traders. As the city's leading merchant, Laclède was among the first to be granted a license. He now enjoyed even greater prosperity, since the licensing reduced competition for furs.

In the early 1770s, not long after the Spanish assumed power in the city, Chouteau became a full

The earliest known map to include St. Louis was drawn by a member of the Spanish military expedition sent to build a fort nearby in 1767. On this map, St. Louis is labeled "Pain-Court," French for "short of bread." The city had earned this nickname because of its occasional food shortages, caused by the fact that farmers were so heavily outnumbered by fur traders there.

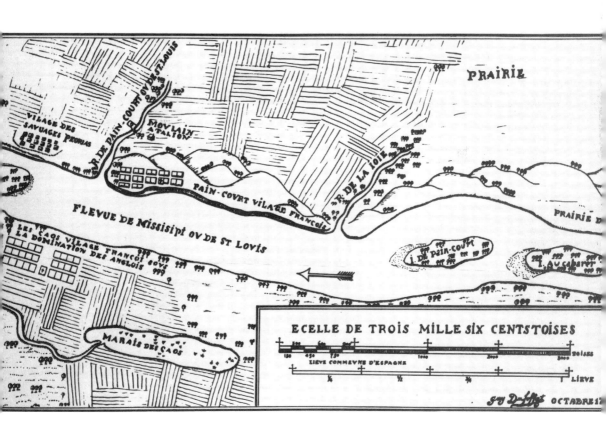

partner in his stepfather's fur-trading business. For much of the next decade, his main job was to assist Laclède in all his business affairs. He helped run the thriving trading headquarters in St. Louis and hired French trappers for expeditions to the fur-trapping grounds. Chouteau also frequently left St. Louis to negotiate trading deals with Native American trappers. In these years, he developed the skills that eventually made him the wealthiest businessman in Missouri.

One of Chouteau's strengths was his ability to negotiate with the Osage Indians and other tribes

In the late eighteenth century, over half the fur trade with Native Americans on the lower Missouri River came from the Osage Indians, which made them especially important to St. Louis businessmen like Laclède and Chouteau.

that lived in the region. He and his half brother, Jean Pierre, who joined the trading firm in the early 1770s, spent long periods of time in Indian villages, learning the Osage language and the tribe's ways and customs. The two brothers knew that success as traders depended as much on treating the Native Americans with respect as it did on striking a hard bargain. They bestowed appropriate gifts on Indian leaders and showed them courtesy and deference. As a result, they themselves were treated with respect and were able to build a thriving business.

Auguste Chouteau would have become a wealthy man before he reached the age of 30, had it not been for his stepfather's financial troubles. Laclède had amassed huge debts in the years when he was expanding his business in New Orleans and in St. Louis. In addition to loans that he had taken to finance his ventures, he had extended credit to a number of businessmen who were later unable to pay him back. By early 1778, Laclède was forced to sell his land holdings and property in St. Louis to a former partner to settle some of his debts.

In a letter written to Chouteau at that time, his stepfather instructed him about the steps he should take in the event of his death. He closed his letter with the words, "Goodbye, my dear sir, I desire to see you again, and to be able myself to settle my affairs. . . . One bequeaths nothing but pain and trouble . . . when one dies poor. Such is my situation." His talk about death was not premature. Just five months later, while on a boat traveling from

Jean Pierre Chouteau (1758-1849), generally known as Pierre, was an important figure on the frontier. Working for Auguste, he extended the fur trade into present-day Oklahoma, establishing the first permanent settlement there in 1796. In 1804, he became the U.S. Indian Agent for the Osage tribe, and in 1809 he and others founded the St. Louis Missouri Fur Company.

New Orleans to St. Louis, Laclède died. He was buried in a spot now long forgotten along the river.

Laclède's death as a poor man was a valuable lesson for 28-year-old Chouteau. It taught him that the only sure way to success was through sound business practices and caution. This was a lesson he would never forget. In the two decades that followed his mentor's death, he focused all his attention and energies on his work and built up a huge business empire of his own.

During those years, Chouteau benefited from the strong ties he had with the Osage Indians. Thanks to this friendship, he was granted a trading monopoly with the tribe. He sent his half brother, Jean Pierre, to act as his representative with the Osage and earned a fortune in the fur trade.

In 1803, when St. Louis became part of the United States as a result of the Louisiana Purchase, Auguste Chouteau was the wealthiest, most powerful man in the region. He offered his services to the American authorities and cooperated in establishing the new government. In 1804, Chouteau was named one of three justices of the first territorial court, and in 1807, he became a colonel in the St. Louis militia. In the following year, when the village of St. Louis was incorporated (legally organized), he was elected chairman of its board of trustees. In 1813, Chouteau became a member of the Legislative Council, part of the governing body of the Missouri Territory. Then, in 1815, he served as a federal commissioner in negotiating treaties with Native Americans in the Missouri region, including the Iowa, Sauk, and Fox tribes.

The Louisiana Purchase

In April 1803, President Thomas Jefferson purchased from France more than 800,000 square miles of land stretching from the Mississippi River to the Rocky Mountains for just a few pennies an acre. Known as the Louisiana Purchase, this land deal more than doubled the size of the United States and made possible the rapid settlement of the region west of the Mississippi.

Although this vast territory had been briefly owned by Spain at the end of the eighteenth century, by 1800 it was once again in French hands, as it had been for many years in the past. Napoleon Bonaparte planned to establish a French empire in the New World, with the Caribbean island of Hispaniola as its capital and the Mississippi River valley its major source of food and trade goods.

In order to build his New World empire, however, Napoleon first had to restore French control in Hispaniola, where slaves under the leadership of Toussaint L'Ouverture had seized power in 1801. In 1802, Napoleon sent a large army to the island. While the French forces won a few battles, they were soon ravaged by disease, and Napoleon was forced to abandon his campaign. Having little use for the Louisiana territory without Hispaniola and in need of money to fund his European adventures, Napoleon offered to sell the huge territory to the United States.

Jefferson, meanwhile, already had negotiators in Paris, working to purchase a tract of land on the lower Mississippi. When the French made their offer to sell the entire Louisiana territory, the American negotiators immediately struck a deal. In an official ceremony held on December 20, 1803, the French formally turned Louisiana over to the United States.

The U.S. flag is raised over New Orleans after the Louisiana Purchase.

By 1818, when this drawing was made, the frontier outpost of St. Louis had been transformed into a peaceful, settled town of several thousand inhabitants.

Even while he was occupied with government service, Chouteau remained involved in his many business interests. He spent most of his time in St. Louis, where he was called "le Colonel Auguste" by the French-speaking residents of the city. Chouteau was the wealthiest citizen and largest landholder in the city he had helped to found. In 1789, he had bought Laclède's original St. Louis trading post and remodeled the crumbling structure into an elegant mansion where he lived with his wife, Thérèse

Cerré—whom he had married in 1786—and four sons and three daughters. The Chouteau home also served as Auguste's business headquarters and even as St. Louis's unofficial community center, hosting visiting dignitaries, social events, political meetings, and even local elections. Auguste Chouteau died in that home on February 24, 1829, at the age of 80.

Although the fur trade declined, St. Louis grew rapidly during the mid-1800s. In 1840, the city's population was 16,000; by 1860, it had risen to 160,000.

Missouri from Territory to Statehood

Until the Osage Indians surrendered their claims to the area in 1808, the only major European settlements in Missouri were St. Louis, Ste. Genevieve, and a few lead mining camps. In 1812, the region was made a U.S. territory, and in the economic boom that followed the War of 1812, settlers began flocking west of the Mississippi River.

Because of its central location and its access to navigable rivers that led to the West, St. Louis became an important departure point for explorers, traders, and settlers. Many of these travelers continued west to the city of Independence, the starting point for both the Santa Fe Trail leading to the southwest and the Oregon Trail leading to the northwest. Thanks to these trails and the traffic they attracted, Missouri's economic future was assured. In 1817, the first steamboat reached St. Louis

on the Mississippi River, launching a new age of travel and trade that drew even more newcomers to the region.

Although many people merely passed through Missouri, others settled there. Planters from the South established wheat and cotton plantations on the rich Missouri lands, bringing their slaves with them. Just a few years later, Missouri's application for admission to the Union as a slave state would add fuel to the growing conflict between North and South. In 1821, Missouri achieved statehood through a special act of Congress known as the Missouri Compromise. This legislation was designed to keep the number of U.S. states permitting slavery equal to the number in which slavery was forbidden. It allowed Maine to join the Union as a free state, while Missouri joined as a slave state.

Chapter Three

Daniel Boone
and the
Settlement of Kentucky

There is no name in the history of frontier America more famous than that of Daniel Boone. Even during his life, he was the stuff of myth and legend. A hunter, Indian fighter, trailblazer, and the founder of two early settlements in southeastern Kentucky, Daniel Boone is, quite simply, one of America's most renowned pioneers.

Daniel Boone was born on November 2, 1734, in a one-room log cabin not far from present-day Reading, Pennsylvania. He was the sixth son of Squire Boone, a weaver, blacksmith, and farmer, and his wife, Sarah.

Even as a boy, Daniel was fascinated by the wilderness. Although he had no formal education, learning little more than how to write his name, he began studying the ways of the outdoorsman early.

Although many popular stories about Daniel Boone (1734-1820) are more folklore than fact, there is no doubt that his courage and determination blazed the way for the settlement of Kentucky.

When Daniel was about 10, his father purchased 25 acres of grazing land several miles from the family homestead. Daniel and his mother spent many long weeks there, watching over the cattle and living off the land while Squire tended to his weaving business in town. Daniel later said that his "love for the wilderness and hunter's life" began with "being a herdsman and thus being so much in the woods." By the age of 13, he was an excellent tracker and marksman. When the Boone family moved, first to the Shenandoah Valley in Virginia and then to the Yadkin River region in western North Carolina, young Daniel regularly went on what were known as "long hunts," extended forays into the wilderness in search of game.

When he was hardly more than a teenager, Daniel joined the Carolina militia and fought as a loyal British subject in the French and Indian War. In early July 1755, he saw action in a terrible battle at Fort Duquesne, the site of present-day Pittsburgh, Pennsylvania. Although he escaped unharmed, 977 of his 2,000 fellow British soldiers were killed or wounded in the fighting.

Following that battle, Daniel returned home and worked on his father's farm in North Carolina. At about that time, he also began courting Rebecca Bryan, the 17-year-old daughter of a neighbor. On August 14, 1756, when Daniel was 21, he and Rebecca were married. The couple's first child, James, was born on May 3, 1757. A second boy, Israel, was born in January 1759. During the next 23 years, Rebecca would give birth to eight more children.

Following his first "long hunt" in 1750, Daniel Boone made a living as a professional hunter of the bear, deer, beaver, otter, and muskrat that were plentiful in North Carolina. The deerskin trade was especially important to the regional economy; in 1753, over 30,000 deerskins were exported from the colony. A hunter like Boone could earn enough from selling skins to buy more gunpowder, bullets, and traps and have plenty of spending money left over.

The French and Indian War

Beginning in 1689, several armed conflicts took place between the French and the English as the two nations battled for control of the vast territory of North America. Typically, each of these conflicts in America was related to a larger war in Europe.

By the mid-1700s, much of the struggle centered on the Ohio River valley. This territory was claimed by both the British and the French and controlled by neither nation. The engagement in which Daniel Boone took part in July 1755 was one of the main battles in the early years of what has come to be known as the French and Indian War. (The French had joined forces with some Native American tribes in their fight against the British.)

Until 1758, the French and their allies enjoyed victory after victory in the war. In that year, Britain sharply increased military aid to the American colonies. The French found it increasingly difficult to continue waging a war far from home. By late 1760, French resistance in North America had virtually ceased. The war came to a formal end in 1763 with the signing of the Treaty of Paris, in which the British gained control of all of North America east of the Mississippi River. This set the stage for the rapid westward expansion of the American colonies.

Native Americans allied with the French attack British troops in one of the many battles of the French and Indian War.

It was the hard work of Rebecca Bryan Boone (1739-1813) that made it possible for her husband to leave home to hunt and explore the new land of Kentucky. Often the sole provider for her children for months at a time, Rebecca not only cooked, cleaned, washed, and sewed, but she also cared for the livestock, planted and harvested the crops, and hunted for small game.

By 1769, Boone was itching to head west before the land was overrun with settlers. He felt crowded in the eastern lands, where game already seemed more scarce. According to one story, when Boone heard that a new family had moved in and was clearing land about 12 miles from his cabin, he said, "The place is getting entirely too thickly settled when a man can come and cut down trees . . . in your backyard!"

Even during the early years of his marriage, Daniel Boone often thought of emigrating westward, to a place the colonists called Kentucky. He'd heard of this wonderful land from John Finley, a fellow soldier in the Carolina militia. As early as 1767, Boone himself had even ventured into the fringes of the territory on some of his "long hunts" in search of game. In the spring of 1769, following the birth of his sixth child, a daughter named Rebecca, he set out to explore deeper into the region where he would ultimately find his greatest fame.

Boone and a party of five men, including Finley, departed from North Carolina on May 1, 1769. The men first made their way north and west until they reached the Cumberland Gap, a great notch in the Appalachian Mountain range that separated the populated southeastern coastal region from the vast unsettled lands of the interior.

From the gap, they traveled north until they reached a spot about two or three miles south of present-day Irvine, Kentucky. There they established a camp. While several of the men stayed behind, Boone and Finley traveled farther north searching for the lands Finley had seen on his earlier visit to the region. Finally, about 20 miles north of their camp, they topped a rise and looked down on a wide expanse of the Kentucky plains.

"We saw with pleasure the beautiful level of Kentucke. We found everywhere abundance of wild beasts of every sort. . . . The buffalo were more frequent than I have seen cattle in the settlements."
—Daniel Boone

Used for centuries by Native Americans, the Cumberland Gap was discovered for the British by Dr. Thomas Walker in 1750.

Kentucky before Boone

More than 12,000 years before Daniel Boone saw the land we know as Kentucky, prehistoric peoples had established civilizations in the region. By the middle of the eighteenth century, Kentucky was home to two Native American tribes. For one of these, the Shawnee, the eastern area of Kentucky was an ancestral homeland.

Austenaco, chief of the Cherokee in 1762

The second great Native American group to inhabit the region was the Cherokee tribe. In prehistoric times, the Cherokee lived in the Great Lakes region. After defeat by the Iroquois and Delaware Indians, the Cherokee moved to the Southeast—into the mountains of the western Carolinas, eastern Tennessee, northern Georgia, and Kentucky. By the time the first Europeans arrived, the Cherokee had become the largest and most powerful Indian nation in the region.

Until the mid-1700s, the Shawnee and the Cherokee lived mostly peaceful lives as farmers and hunters. All that changed in 1750, when Dr. Thomas Walker, an early explorer, discovered the Cumberland Gap: a natural pass through the Cumberland Mountains that provided an easy route to the Kentucky frontier. In 1768, Iroquois Indians—who did not live in the area—ceded the Kentucky lands to the British. The Iroquois claimed Kentucky was theirs to give because, during wars in the previous century, they had defeated the tribes that lived there. Eager for new areas to settle, the British began to move in. Not surprisingly, however, the Shawnee and Cherokee tribes saw pioneers like Daniel Boone as trespassers on their rightful territory, a disagreement that would lead to bloody conflict in the years to come.

For almost two years, the men hunted and trapped in what is known as the "bluegrass" country of Kentucky. They were constantly amazed by the animal life they saw. Buffalo, deer, and elk were thick in the wild lands. During these years, Boone and his companions had several run-ins with the Shawnee Indians, for whom Kentucky was a homeland and favorite hunting ground.

When he returned to North Carolina in May 1771, Boone found increased interest in settling Kentucky. The population in the eastern colonies was growing, and there was a steady press of people moving westward. In mid-1773, Boone led a group of about 50 settlers—including his wife, his children,

In George Caleb Bingham's 1851-1852 oil painting Daniel Boone Escorting Settlers through the Cumberland Gap, *Boone is portrayed as a noble, heroic leader bringing his family and other settlers through the dark and forbidding mountains.*

and his brother Squire's family—into Kentucky in what was the first formal attempt to establish a settlement on the frontier. The effort failed, however, following an attack by a party of Delaware, Cherokee, and Shawnee Indians. Boone's eldest son, James, was killed in the raid, which terrified most of the would-be settlers.

Following this attack and answering violence on the part of the settlers pushing westward from Virginia and the Carolinas, full-scale war broke out between Indians and settlers in Kentucky. Faced by overwhelming odds, the Native Americans, including members of the Shawnee and Delaware tribes, surrendered in the autumn of 1774. After peace was declared, Boone was ready once again to try and establish a settlement in the West.

By this time, Richard Henderson, a land speculator from North Carolina, had turned his full attention to the settlement of the Kentucky territory. Aware of Boone's reputation as a frontiersman, Henderson hired him to lead a group of men into the wilderness to clear a path for settlers.

In mid-March 1775, Boone gathered a company of about 35 men who had volunteered to help him hack out a road from Tennessee into Kentucky. This group included Daniel's brother Squire, who had come from North Carolina with a number of Boone's friends. Also included in the group were two women: Susannah, Daniel's 14-year-old daughter, and a slave woman. It was their job to cook for the party and maintain the camp.

The Native Americans of Kentucky were particularly angry that the white men entering their territory were professional hunters whose methods—killing a great number of animals, taking the valuable skins, and leaving much of the meat to rot—the Indians considered wasteful and disrespectful.

Leaving Tennessee, Boone led his party through the Cumberland Gap and into the wilds of Kentucky. He made use of "buffalo roads," tracks made by the shaggy beasts as they lumbered through the forest. "Buffaloes made the road," one of the earliest Kentucky pioneers later remarked, "Boone marked it."

While Boone's expedition followed the buffalo roads, the route was not an easy one. The men had to chop down saplings and remove underbrush to widen and level the path so that settlers traveling in wagons could follow in their footsteps. The path that they carved out later became known as the Wilderness Road, sometimes called Boone's Trace.

Boone's party spent two weeks hacking and chopping their way through almost untouched woods. Then, on March 22, they got their first glimpse of what Felix Walker, one of the road builders, described as the "pleasing and rapturous appearance of the plains of Kentucky . . . [where] a new sky and strange earth seemed to be presented to our view."

Near the end of their journey, the Boone party made camp on March 24. There they awaited the arrival of a large group—about two dozen mounted riflemen and a handful of settlers—being led by Henderson over the road that Boone and his companions had just cleared. On the night of March 25, before Henderson and his men arrived, the Boone party was attacked by a group of Indians, probably Cherokee. Several men were killed, and a second attack just a few days later killed two more.

Boone blazed the Wilderness Road from the Cumberland Gap to the south bank of the Kentucky River, but it eventually connected to other roads that ran as far east as Virginia and as far west as Louisville, Kentucky. The road later was widened to accommodate wagons, and hundreds of thousands of pioneers traveled it on their journey to the West. Although the road was abandoned in the 1840s, it survives today as part of U.S. Route 25, known as the Dixie Highway.

Although Fort Boonesborough remained a trading center for the next 50 years, its population steadily declined as the need for defense against the Indians and the British decreased. By 1820, Boonesborough had ceased to exist as a town. The fort has been reconstructed and is now part of a state park.

After dispatching a letter to Henderson asking him to hurry with his riflemen, Boone and his companions moved about 15 miles north from their camp. There, in a clearing on the Kentucky River's south shore, they quickly threw together a collection of log huts.

Henderson, who arrived in early April, had lofty plans for the community that the settlers dubbed Boonesborough. He ordered the building of a large log fort about 200 feet from the river and

placed Boone in charge of its construction, but work went slowly. Though there was a total of about 80 men at the new settlement, most were busy staking out their own claims, planting crops, or hunting for skins and meat. By summer, Boone was able to oversee the building of a small powder magazine (a place to store ammunition) and two small blockhouses (military fortifications). The rest of Henderson's planned fort was constructed piece by piece, and one settler arriving several months after Boonesborough was established reported that he saw only a handful of log cabins scattered about the countryside near the blockhouses.

Boone stayed in the tiny settlement that was named in his honor until the autumn of 1775, when he returned to North Carolina. There, he gathered his family and a party of about two dozen young frontiersmen and led them to Boonesborough. During the next several years, as the 13 original colonies began their fight for independence from Britain, Boone was kept busy in Kentucky. He hunted, surveyed the lands around Boonesborough, and engaged in an endless series of scrapes with the Native Americans of the region, some of whom had allied themselves with the British against the colonists.

While Boonesborough never thrived as a settlement, it did survive, thanks largely to Boone's efforts. During the period following its establishment, he played a central role in defending the fort and the settlers from a number of Indian attacks. Meanwhile, Boone's fame was spreading far beyond

Boone's position in the Revolutionary War was ambiguous. His wife's family, the Bryans, were staunch Loyalists (supporters of the British). He, however, favored independence. According to one of his descendants, Boone found the Bryans' Loyalist sympathies "one of the most trying things he ever met with, to see some of his best friends so carried away in so bad a cause." Perhaps as a way to keep his wife happy, he—like many Kentuckians— followed a moderate course, fighting only when it was necessary to protect his family and his community.

On July 14, 1776, 13-year-old Jemima Boone and two of her friends, Elizabeth and Frances Calloway, were kidnapped by Cherokee and Shawnee Indians while canoeing on the Kentucky River. As the girls used ingenious tricks to try to delay their captors, Daniel Boone led a search party in pursuit, finally managing to rescue the prisoners three days later. "Thank Almighty Providence, boys, for we have the girls safe," he exclaimed upon being reunited with his daughter. "Let's all sit down by them now and have a hearty cry."

Kentucky, due to exploits that seem almost too fantastic to be believed.

On February 9, 1778, for example, Boone and a party of about 30 men left the fort on an expedition to find salt and were captured by the Shawnee. They were taken about 100 miles north to an Indian village and held prisoner. They lived with the Indians until about four months later, when Boone discovered that the Shawnee—working in league with the British—were preparing to attack Boonesborough. He slipped away from his captors, stole a horse, and rode south. When the horse gave out, he took off on foot, disguising his trail by running through riverbeds, along fallen trees, and over rocks until he reached the Ohio River.

At the river, he found a fallen log that would serve as a raft. Taking with him some ammunition and a rifle he had fashioned from parts stolen from the Indians, he floated downstream on the log until he reached Kentucky. When Boone made his way to Boonesborough on June 20, 1778, he found his cabin empty. Rebecca and the children, thinking him dead, had returned home to North Carolina.

Soon after his escape, Boone played an important part in defending Boonesborough when the Shawnee and British, as expected, attacked the settlement. After helping the settlers ward off the attack in September 1778, he made his way back to North Carolina to rejoin his wife and children. A year later, though, he was again on the trail through the Cumberland Gap, leading yet another band of settlers into the Kentucky wilderness. Rather than stopping at Boonesborough, however, Boone led about 100 men, women, and children—including his own family—to a spot about six miles northwest of the settlement. There he helped establish a new settlement known as Boone's Station.

It was late in the season when Boone and the 20 families with him arrived at the chosen spot. They quickly built rough-hewn dwellings to provide shelter. Though that first winter was terrible, most of the hardy settlers survived. With the coming of spring, Boone's Station began taking shape as men built sturdy cabins and a small fort for protection against Indian attack.

Boone himself soon moved to a spot about two miles from the settlement, where he built a large

The first winter in Boone's Station was, according to one Kentuckian, "as severely cold" as any he had experienced. Indeed, it became known as the Hard Winter. Livestock died in the field and wild turkeys froze to death on their perches in the forest. The bitter cold made it almost impossible for the settlers to hunt for food, and many "did actuly Die for the want of solid food." Boone, who brought a good supply of corn with him from North Carolina, shared the grain with the others in his party.

cabin. This would be home to him and his family: his wife, Rebecca, their eldest son, Israel, their two younger daughters, Levina and Rebecca, and two younger sons, Daniel Morgan and Jesse. (Boone's two eldest daughters, Jemima and Susannah, had married pioneer men and lived in Boone's Station.) It was at this home, in 1781, that Rebecca gave birth to the couple's tenth and last child, Nathan. Also living with the Boones during this time were six motherless children of one of Rebecca's uncles and a family of five who were Daniel's friends. All told, the household near Boone's Station numbered about 20 people.

During the next several years, Boone continued hunting while family members farmed corn and tobacco and tended horses and cattle. Eventually, he turned more and more of his attention to land speculation. Boone bought claims to about 1,400 acres in Kentucky. He also became involved with a group of investors who entrusted him with about $20,000 to be used to purchase land in the city of Williamsburg, Virginia. On his way to make the purchase, however, Boone was robbed—perhaps by an innkeeper who drugged him and stole the money while he slept.

The theft of the money was, for Boone, a disaster. He spent several years struggling to pay back the funds he had been given by the investors. The loss also affected his spirits, leaving him feeling weak and vulnerable as he never had when facing the dangers of the frontier.

Although Boone lost confidence following this disaster, many of his fellow settlers continued to trust

After Boone was robbed of the $20,000, rumors spread that he staged the theft to pocket the money himself. One of his friends, Thomas Hart, wrote in Boone's defense: "I feel . . . for poor Boone whose Character I am told Suffers by [the theft]. Much degenerated must the people of this Age be, when Amoungst them are to be found men to Censure and Blast the Character and Reputation of a person So Just and Upright. . . . I have known Boone in times of Old, when Poverty and distress had him fast by the hand, And . . . I ever found him of a Noble and generous Soul despising every thing mean."

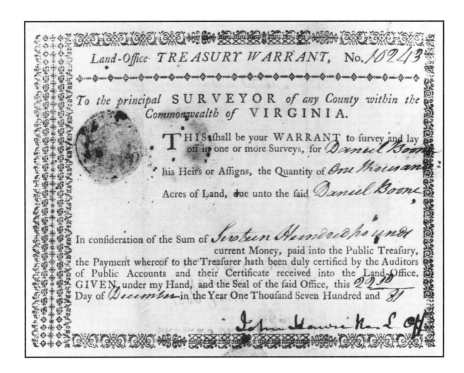

Land-Office TREASURY WARRANT, No. *10243*

To the principal SURVEYOR of any County within the Commonwealth of VIRGINIA.

THIS shall be your WARRANT to survey and lay off in one or more Surveys, for *Daniel Boone* his Heirs or Assigns, the Quantity of *One Thousand* Acres of Land, due unto the said *Daniel Boone*,

In consideration of the Sum of *Sixteen Hundred pounds* current Money, paid into the Public Treasury, the Payment whereof to the Treasurer hath been duly certified by the Auditors of Public Accounts and their Certificate received into the Land-Office. GIVEN, under my Hand, and the Seal of the said Office, this *22d* Day of *December* in the Year One Thousand Seven Hundred and *81*

A treasury warrant granting Boone a claim to 1,000 acres of land in Kentucky (then part of Virginia). Buying treasury warrants was like gambling: if anyone else demonstrated a prior claim, Boone would lose the land and the money he paid for the warrant (in this case, 1,600 pounds).

and respect him. He was elected to several public offices over the next few years, including the job of representing Kentucky (which had become a county of Virginia in 1776) in the Virginia State Assembly.

During this period, conflict between the westward-pushing settlers and the Native Americans who were being forced off their lands was almost constant. The Indians of Kentucky and Ohio fought bravely, but they lost more and more land to the overpowering forces of the settlers. Boone was involved in a few battles himself, including a terrible fight between Shawnee warriors and a volunteer militia in Ohio in early 1780. Later that same year, as he and his brother Edward were hunting near Boone's Station, Edward was killed in a surprise attack.

Blue Licks and the Licking River were named for the abundant salt deposits (licks) found nearby. The licks not only made good hunting spots (because animals gathered to feed on the salt), but they also provided settlers with salt for seasoning and preserving food.

After suffering heavy losses, the settlers ended the Battle of Blue Licks with a retreat.

So far in his life, Boone had lost his eldest son, James, his brother Edward, and several of his close friends to Indian attacks. And there were more losses to come in the seemingly endless skirmishes and battles with the Native Americans. In 1782, Indians made several raids in response to brutal attacks by settlers. A large force, with Boone as one of its leaders, was sent to overpower the Native Americans in the area between Boonesborough and the Ohio River. This group made a foolhardy attack on an even larger force of Indians at a spot called Blue Licks, on the Licking River. Boone himself was one of the men responsible for initiating the attack, which took the life of his son Israel.

By 1784, with the end of the Revolutionary War, the western frontier—including Kentucky—began to be flooded with immigrants. Boone, then 50 years old, was ready to settle down, or at least to spend less time in the wilderness. Not long after the war's end, he and his family settled in Limestone, a small town on the west bank of the Ohio River just northwest of Blue Licks. In Limestone (today Maysville), he became a leading citizen. At about this time, Boone's fame increased with the publication of a book about the settlement of Kentucky written by John Filson, which included a section on "The Adventures of Col. Daniel Boon." This account—as much myth as fact—made Boone's name known not only across America but in Europe as well. The English poet George Gordon, Lord Byron, even included Boone and his exploits in his long poem *Don Juan*.

The years immediately after Boone moved to Limestone were relatively peaceful. He continued trying his hand at land speculation, but lost more money than he earned. He soon found himself with debts he couldn't pay and in legal hot water because he sold lands for which he did not have clear claims. These legal problems hounded him for much of the rest of his life.

During these years, a formal peace existed between the settlers and the Indians of the Kentucky region, but there were constant skirmishes between the two groups. In 1786, as an officer in the frontier militia, Boone took part in what would be his last major battle—a bloody attack on a Shawnee village.

John Filson (1747-1788) has often been criticized for his romanticized version of Boone's life. Boone himself, however, declared upon reading it, "All true! Every word true! Not a lie in it."

"My footsteps have often been marked with blood. Two darling sons, and a brother, have I lost by savage hands. . . . Many dark and sleepless nights have I been a companion for owls, separated from the chearful society of men, scorched by the Summer's sun, and pinched by the Winter's cold. . . . This delightful country [Kentucky] . . . I have seen purchased with a vast expence of blood and treasure."
—Daniel Boone, as told to John Filson

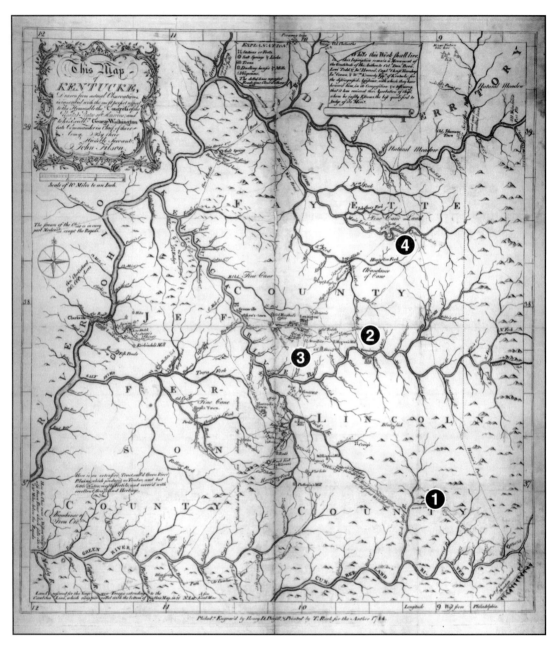

A 1784 map of Kentucky by John Filson. Among the landmarks are the Wilderness Road (1), Boonesborough (2), Boone's house (3), and Blue Licks (4).

Later, he helped to arrange a prisoner exchange between the Native Americans and the settlers.

Two years later, Boone, Rebecca, Daniel Morgan, Jesse, and Nathan relocated to Point Pleasant, West Virginia, where Boone began shipping goods to and from Limestone. His bad luck as a businessman continued and, in 1792, he was forced to abandon his business. Though he was nearing 60, he and his family moved yet again, to a cabin near present-day Charleston, West Virginia.

This move, and the fact that he was, for his time, an old man, marked a major turning point in

Thomas Cole's 1826 painting Daniel Boone at His Cabin at Great Osage Lake *portrays the elderly Boone as a lonely figure overwhelmed by and isolated from the wilderness around him.*

Boone's life. For the rest of his years, Boone seemed to have no place in the wilderness he loved. He and Rebecca, living alone now, moved several times as Boone's health began to fail. He suffered from rheumatism and left most of the hunting chores to younger men while he set and tended beaver traps.

Finally, in 1799, Boone turned his back on the Kentucky lands once and for all. He, Rebecca, and several members of what had become a large extended family moved to Missouri, where Boone's sons Daniel Morgan and Nathan had settled. There, in 1803, Boone was injured when his hand was caught in a steel trap. He was forced to give up hunting completely, and he and Rebecca relied more and more heavily upon their children.

Boone's waning years were marred by legal troubles that arose from his business dealings. He was sued and found responsible for faulty land claims he filed. During these years, too, death visited his family several times. Not long after the family's arrival in Missouri, Boone's daughter Susannah died. Her death was followed, in 1803, by the death of another daughter, Levina. Two years later, Rebecca, his youngest daughter, also died. The greatest blow to strike him, however, was the death in 1813 of his wife, Rebecca, the woman he had courted and married some 50 years before.

During these years, Boone's health grew worse and worse, though he still was able to hunt occasionally. After Rebecca's death, he began living with his only surviving daughter, Jemima, in a house near the burial ground where his wife had been laid to rest. Thoughts of his own death weighed heavily on his mind, and he even went so far as to have his coffin made in 1816, when he was in his 80s. On September 26, 1820, the death that Boone seemed to be anxiously awaiting came. Nathan and Jemima were at his bedside not long after sunrise on that day. "I am going," he said. "My time has come."

Kentucky after Boone

During Daniel Boone's lifetime, Kentucky's population grew rapidly and larger settlements were formed, including one at Louisville in 1778 and one at Frankfort (which would later become the capital) in 1786. Both the Shawnee and Cherokee tribes had the misfortune to stand in the way of this great migration of Europeans from the eastern seaboard into the western frontier. While they resisted the settlers, they were unable to stop the flow of newcomers into what had long been their hunting grounds. Eventually the Shawnee were driven from their lands, first to Indiana, then farther west, with most ending up on reservations in what is now Oklahoma. The Cherokee, too, were driven from their homes and forced onto reservations in present-day Oklahoma.

As settlers gradually overran Kentucky, there was increased pressure for the region to become a state. The first constitution was approved in April 1792, and, just over a month later, Kentucky became the 15th state to join the Union. Following its entry into the United States, the pace of settlement in Kentucky increased dramatically. Between 1792 and the outbreak of the Civil War in 1861, the state's population grew from about 75,000 to more than 1 million.

Though slavery was widespread in Kentucky, the state did not secede from the Union and tried to remain neutral during the Civil War. But neutrality was hard to maintain, largely because of the state's strategic location bordering both the Ohio and Mississippi Rivers. To gain access to those rivers, the Confederate Army invaded Kentucky soon after the start of the war. Fighting was over by 1863, however, after Union troops drove the Confederates from the state.

Chapter Four

John Sevier
and the
Founding of Tennessee

O n a July day early in the Revolutionary War, a frontier fort in the area that is now the state of Tennessee came under attack by a group of Cherokee and Chickamauga Indians fighting on the side of the British. The attack came at daybreak, when a number of women were outside the fort tending to livestock. Suddenly, the air was filled with war cries as Native American warriors streamed from the woods.

The women, terrified, fled for the safety of the fort. One, a young woman named Catherine Sherrill, was intercepted by the Indian attackers. Somehow, she managed to evade them, but when she reached the fort, she saw that the gates had been closed. She made a huge leap and managed to grab the top of the wall surrounding the fort. Hearing

As a frontiersman, a soldier, and a politician, John Sevier (1745-1815) fought passionately for the freedom and prosperity of early Tennessee.

her screams, John Sevier, a young man who was second-in-command at the fort that day, came to her aid. With a pistol in one hand, he sprang to the top of the wall to help Catherine over. Sevier shot her closest pursuer and pulled the terrified young woman to safety inside the fort. His bravery that day made him famous along the frontier. Sevier was later elected as Tennessee's first governor, and he is honored as one of the state's true pioneer founders.

John Sevier was born on September 23, 1745, near what is now the town of New Market, in the Shenandoah Valley region of Virginia. He was the first of seven children of Valentine and Joanna Sevier. Valentine was a farmer and also owned a small country store. As a boy, John helped his father work the family farm. At that time, the Shenandoah Valley was the wild country of America's frontier, an area where turkey, deer, and other game abounded. Growing up there, young John learned to hunt and became an excellent shot.

John's schooling was limited. Like many frontier boys, he first attended what was known as a "field school," a one-room log schoolhouse. There, he learned a little spelling and writing, some grammar, and just enough arithmetic to add and subtract. For a time, he attended Staunton Academy (the equivalent of a modern-day high school), located not far from his home. He must have been a good student, at least when it came to writing and spelling. His later correspondence shows that he mastered the skills necessary to compose a well-written letter. School, however, did not much interest John Sevier.

When he was about 16 years of age, he left Staunton and started working in his father's store. Soon after that, in 1761, he married a neighbor girl, Sarah Hawkins.

During the next several years, Sevier worked as a farmer, an innkeeper, and a merchant. While still in his twenties, he was one of the region's most successful men, wealthy enough to donate three acres of land to the Baptist congregation in New Market so that its members could build a new church.

Sevier's family, meanwhile, was growing rapidly. By the early 1770s, he and Sarah had six or perhaps seven children. Like most parents, Sevier wanted to provide a good future for his children. Probably for that reason, he decided to leave New Market for the remote frontier of what is now eastern Tennessee, where land was plentiful and cheap.

As early as 1771, Sevier explored the region south of the Shenandoah Valley. Just north of the Holston and Watauga Rivers in present-day Tennessee, he found what was to his mind an ideal location to start a new life: a land with rich soil, filled with wild game. He visited this region, known as the Watauga District, again the following year and then, sometime in early 1773, built a cabin about a mile north of the Holston River. Then he headed back to Virginia to gather up his family.

Sevier's description of the land he had found must have made it sound like paradise. As soon as he told the other members of the Sevier family in Virginia of his plans to move, all of them decided to travel to the Watauga region along with him. On

December 25, 1773, 28-year-old John Sevier, his relatives, and all their belongings arrived in the frontier town of Holston, a few miles north of the Holston River in what is now Tennessee. In the group were John's own wife and children, his parents, his four brothers, Robert, Joseph, Valentine, and Abraham, and his two sisters, Polly and Catherine.

After moving to the Watauga District, Sevier quickly settled into life on the frontier. Like other frontiersmen of his time, he wore buckskin shoes, leggings that reached above his knees, short pantaloons, and a hunting shirt, probably of deerskin. A belt at his waist held a knife and a tomahawk.

Sevier and his family lived in a log cabin, as did all the settlers at the time. We don't know exactly what this home was like, but it's safe to assume it was like most cabins on the frontier—crude, but strong enough to withstand attacks by Indians who resented the newcomers moving into lands they had occupied for generations. Its walls would have had round holes through which the occupants could shoot flintlock muskets in case of an attack. The cabin's floors and doors would have been made of thick planks hewn from local trees; its glassless windows would be covered by shutters. At one end of the cabin's main room, there would have been a large fireplace with a chimney made of wattle and daub (sticks covered with mud to prevent fires). The furniture was almost surely made by Sevier himself, though there may have been a piece or two brought from England when the family originally came to America.

Tennessee before Sevier

The earliest known inhabitants of Tennessee were the prehistoric Native American people now known as mound builders. A few of these people were still living in the region when the Spanish explorer Hernando de Soto became the first European to explore what is now Tennessee in 1541. French explorers followed, traveling down the Mississippi River and claiming the surrounding lands for France. By the time Robert de La Salle built Fort Prudhomme near the site of present-day Memphis in about 1682, the last mound builders had been wiped out by warfare and disease brought to the region by the Europeans.

In John Sevier's time, three major Native American tribes lived in Tennessee. The Cherokee, who spoke an Iroquois language, inhabited what is now eastern Tennessee. This Native American tribe—once the greatest in the southeastern United States—had, by Sevier's time, been gravely weakened by a smallpox epidemic that killed half of its members. The Cherokee, however, still had a powerful and advanced culture. The Shawnee, one of a number of Algonquian-speaking tribes in North America, lived in central Tennessee.

The Chickasaw, the most warlike of the three tribes in Tennessee, spoke a Muskogean language and lived in the western part of the region.

In the mid-1700s, both the French and the English became interested in establishing control of Tennessee. Eventually, both nations claimed parts of the region. The British established their first settlement west of the Smoky Mountains at Fort Loudoun in 1756, but the soldiers stationed there were massacred four years later by Cherokee Indians and the fort was abandoned. In 1763, following its defeat in the French and Indian War, France gave up its claims to all its lands east of the Mississippi River, including Tennessee, to England. Soon interest in founding permanent settlements in Tennessee began to increase, much to the resentment of the area's Native American inhabitants. Though they frequently waged war in an attempt to stop the theft of their land, by about 1840 virtually all of Tennessee's Native Americans had been killed or relocated to reservations in the West. Ironically, the name "Tennessee" was adapted from *Tanasi*, the name of Cherokee villages in the region.

Tecumseh (1768-1813), chief of the Shawnee during much of Sevier's time in Tennessee, is famous for organizing and leading a great confederacy of Native American tribes against the white settlers. This effort was defeated in 1811 at the Battle of Tippecanoe in Indiana.

After settling in the Watauga District, Sevier soon became one of its leading residents. He had pleasant manners that quickly turned strangers into friends. He founded a country store, which prospered as immigrants flocked to the area in search of cheap land and opportunity. Sevier took an active role in local affairs when he became one of the leaders of a group known as the Watauga Association. This group had been formed in 1772 to provide a form of self-government for the Watauga District and protection for its residents.

As the number of settlers moving to the western frontier steadily increased during the early 1770s, the Shawnee Indians who lived in the area grew resentful of the newcomers they viewed as land thieves. In late 1773, the Native Americans made their resentment known when they attacked a party of settlers that Daniel Boone was leading to Kentucky. The next year, the conflict grew worse when several land surveyors were killed.

The violence increased as European settlers moving into the region committed terrible acts against the Shawnee and Cherokee Indians. The Native Americans responded by attacking settlers and killing as many as they could. By late 1774, war was raging along the frontier. This conflict has come to be known as Lord Dunmore's War, named for the British governor of Virginia.

John Sevier apparently had attracted Lord Dunmore's attention, probably because he was a community leader. In October 1774, Dunmore, recognizing Sevier's leadership ability, appointed him a

John Murray (1730-1809), the fourth earl of Dunmore, was the British governor of Virginia from 1771 to 1775. In 1774, in an attempt to expand Britain's influence in America and to put an end to Indian attacks on settlers, he fought and defeated the Shawnee Indians in what became known as Lord Dunmore's War. Unpopular with most colonial settlers, Dunmore was forced to take refuge on a British warship when the American Revolution began in 1775.

captain in the Virginia militia. During the war, he and his men defended the Watauga settlement.

Even as the settlers of the Watauga region were waging war against the Indians, tension between the American colonies and Britain was increasing. In April 1775, that tension grew into open warfare with the battles of Lexington and Concord. The American Revolution had begun.

Sevier was an ardent supporter of the colonists during the Revolutionary War. In July 1776, he displayed his bravery during the defense of Fort Watauga against the attack of Native Americans allied with the British. It was during this conflict that Sevier rescued Catherine Sherrill, an episode that made him famous along the frontier.

Not long after the attack on the fort, the members of the Watauga Association displayed their unity with the colonists now at war with Britain by renaming their region the Washington District, in honor of General George Washington. At about the same time, the 600 or so residents of the district, including Sevier, sent a petition to the colonial government of North Carolina, asking it to extend its jurisdiction over the region. That petition was soon granted, and the Washington District became Washington County, North Carolina. In short order, Sevier was elected as one of three delegates to represent the county at the constitutional convention in Halifax, North Carolina, in late 1776.

During the next several years, Sevier continued to serve as one of the leaders in the continuing struggle with the Indians fighting on the British side in the Revolutionary War. He shared the leadership of the Watauga region with James Robertson, another famous Tennessee pioneer. When Robertson left

Virginian James Robertson (1742-1814) is considered one of the great founders of Tennessee. In 1772, he led groups of settlers into what is now east Tennessee and helped to organize the Watauga Association. Robertson brought other settlers farther west in 1780, founding a community at the site of the present-day city of Nashville and serving for a time as head of the local government.

the area and moved west in 1780, Sevier became the most important of the eastern Tennessee pioneers.

In the autumn of 1780, the British decided to bring the Revolutionary War to the Watauga region, which was, by that time, a hotbed of rebel activities. Lord Cornwallis, one of the British generals, sent an expeditionary force to the region under the leadership of Lieutenant Colonel Patrick Ferguson. Ferguson's orders were to subdue the colonial sympathizers.

In late September 1780, Sevier, then a colonel in charge of the Washington County militia, learned of the British plans. He immediately contacted other leaders of the frontier militias, including Isaac Shelby, colonel of the militia in nearby Sullivan County, and made plans to turn back the British forces.

A large force of backwoodsman and farmers, often called "overmountain men," gathered to defend the Watauga region against the British.

Soon an army of almost 1,000 backwoodsmen, including 240 recruited and commanded by Sevier, headed across the Great Smoky Mountains to King's Mountain, on the border between North and South Carolina. There, on October 6, the colonists confronted the British in a terrible battle. Sevier and his men were in the middle of the action and withstood several bayonet charges and intense hand-to-hand fighting. Finally, they captured the battlefield's high ground and forced the British to raise the white flag of surrender.

There was more to Sevier's life, however, than battles and warfare. In 1778, he and his family had moved south from Watauga to the southern banks of the Nolichucky River. There he built a log mansion large enough to house himself, his wife, Sarah, and his 10 children—Joseph, James, John, Valentine, Richard, Betsey, Dolly, Mary Ann, Nancy, and Rebecca. For a time, life at Mount Pleasant, as he named his estate, was very pleasant. Then, in early 1780, Sarah, the woman he had married almost two decades earlier, died.

Sevier soon realized he needed a companion who could help him care for his children. A short time after Sarah's death, he began courting Catherine Sherrill, the young woman he had rescued at Fort Watauga during the Indian attack in 1776. In September 1780, they were married in a ceremony performed by a justice of the peace. "Bonny Kate," as Sevier called her, appears to have truly loved her frontier hero. She often said that she would gladly endure another chase and would happily leap a fort's walls in order to enjoy such an introduction again. During the years of their happy marriage, Catherine and John Sevier would have eight children—Ruth, Catherine, George Washington, Joanna Goade, Samuel, Robert, Polly Preston, and Elizabeth Conway.

Sevier's military activities were hardly slowed by his marriage to Bonny Kate. Immediately after returning from the Battle of King's Mountain in 1780, he led his men on a campaign against the Cherokee Indians, who continued to aid the British by harassing the frontier settlements. In the next few years, Sevier saw steady action against the Native Americans of east Tennessee. In one battle, he fought alongside Francis Marion, the "Swamp Fox" whose guerrilla warfare tactics earned him fame during the Revolutionary War.

Francis Marion (1732-1795) was a frontiersman and Indian fighter. As a lieutenant colonel in the Continental Army during the Revolutionary War, he led an attack on British-held Savannah, Georgia, in 1779. Later in the war, Marion became the leader of a small guerrilla band that took refuge in the Carolina swamps when faced by overwhelming British forces. It was at this time that he became famous as the "Swamp Fox."

Immediately following the end of the war in 1783, thousands of new settlers moved into Tennessee to what was then the western frontier of the new nation. Land was plentiful and, with the British gone and the Native Americans in the region largely defeated in battle, the territory was an attractive place to settle. Sevier, famous by this time for his exploits as an Indian fighter and frontier patriot, became a land speculator. He hoped to profit from the influx of settlers into the settlements along the Watauga and Holston Rivers.

In mid-1784, North Carolina passed legislation ceding its western counties, including all the land we now know as Tennessee, to the Continental Congress (the governing body established by the colonies after the Revolutionary War). This action was the state's way of paying off the heavy war debts it owed to the central government. Under the terms of the agreement, the Continental Congress had two years to decide whether to accept or reject North Carolina's gift. During those two years, the state would retain jurisdiction over the Tennessee region.

Sevier and many other residents of Tennessee had long felt neglected by North Carolina, which had taxed them without providing any services, such as roads or military protection. They had not been consulted before their lands were ceded, and they believed that the region would suffer during the two-year waiting period, when it would be neither a real part of North Carolina nor under the control of the Continental Congress. Something had to be done.

It was not long before Sevier was in the fore-
front of a movement to create a government that
would truly represent the people of Tennessee.
Following meetings in late 1784 and early 1785,
Washington, Sullivan, and Greene counties declared
themselves the independent state of Franklin. John
Sevier was named governor of the new state, which
was named after Benjamin Franklin.

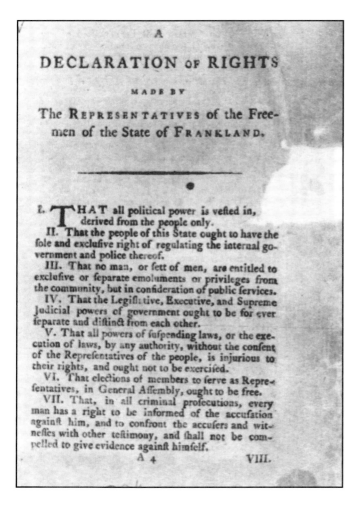

*The Franklin Declaration of
Rights was the preamble to the
Franklin Constitution,
written in 1784.*

The government of North Carolina opposed the formation of a state by its western counties, as did a minority of the residents of the region. Eventually, the resistance of this minority grew into open conflict between forces loyal to Sevier and an anti-Franklin faction led by a settler named John Tipton. On at least one occasion, Sevier and Tipton had a fistfight that was, luckily, broken up before either man was hurt.

During the next several years, Sevier and his followers, known as "Franks," continued trying unsuccessfully to gain recognition for Franklin as one of the states of the Union. During these years, the legislature of North Carolina passed an act that declared that the western counties would, at some later date, be formed into an independent state if they gave up their fight immediately and waited for the law to take its course. At the same time, pardons were offered to all who turned their backs on Sevier and the Franks. Many settlers, tired of the strife, took the deal offered by the North Carolinians. By late 1787, it was clear that Franklin would never be accepted into the Union.

Suddenly, at the age of 43, Sevier went from being a hero to being a wanted criminal. Since he personally never accepted the pardon offered by North Carolina, he was considered a traitor. A warrant was issued for his arrest.

To escape capture, Sevier fled to the far western frontier with a band of followers. Desperate to find some way to guarantee the success of Franklin, he flirted with the idea of placing the region under

When it failed to be recognized as a state of the Union, Franklin attempted to become an independent nation. It decided to build a mint and produce its own coins—although it is not certain whether it ever did so, since no Franklin money has survived. In the meantime, taxes and the salaries of government officials were paid in goods; as governor, Sevier received 1,000 deerskins per year.

the protection of the Spanish government. (At this time, Spain controlled large parts of North America west of the Mississippi River.) Finally, in July 1788, North Carolina's governor had Sevier arrested on charges of treason against the state. He was taken to the town of Morgantown, near the Tennessee-North Carolina border, but the frontiersman and Indian fighter was rescued by friends and never stood trial.

Meanwhile, the United States Constitution was ratified by a majority of the thirteen colonies in 1787. Though North Carolina had not yet ratified the federal constitution, it was obvious that the former colony would soon become a state. In early 1789, in an attempt to bring the Franklin controversy to an end, the North Carolina government again offered pardons to all Franks. This time, Sevier accepted the offer and took the oath of loyalty to North Carolina.

Once Sevier accepted the fact that Franklin no longer existed, he became a strong supporter of statehood for North Carolina. In November 1789, delegates from around North Carolina attended a state convention. At that time, Sevier was elected to the North Carolina Senate, fully pardoned, and restored to his rank as brigadier general in the North Carolina militia. He, along with the majority of senators, voted in favor of ratifying the federal constitution. For the next two years, Sevier served as the representative of North Carolina's western district in the U.S. Congress.

In late 1790, North Carolina's earlier decision to cede its western counties to the federal government

Sevier became involved in what is called the "Spanish conspiracy," an attempt to convince western settlers to secede from the United States and join with Spain, which offered large tracts of land in Spanish territory, access to trade on the Mississippi River, and better trade relations with the Native Americans. Ultimately, however, nothing came of this project.

"When they delivered [my father] to the jailer at Morgantown, who had fought at King's Mountain, [the jailer] knocked off the irons from his hands and told him to go where he please, not, however, to leave the place. [Sevier's rescuers] . . . found Colonel Sevier . . . [and] told him frankly they had come for him and that he must go. . . . Without any fear from the jailer or any one else, Colonel Sevier ordered his horse and all started off . . . in the most open and public manner, and returned home."
—John Sevier Jr.

took effect. At that time, the lands that would eventually be Tennessee became the "Territory of the United States South of the River Ohio." Settlers hungry for land and opportunity poured into the new territory. By November 1795, there were 60,000 residents, the number needed to apply to the federal government for statehood. Each county elected five delegates to a constitutional convention

Settlers thronging to Tennessee built forts like the Knoxville Blockhouse, shown here in about 1793.

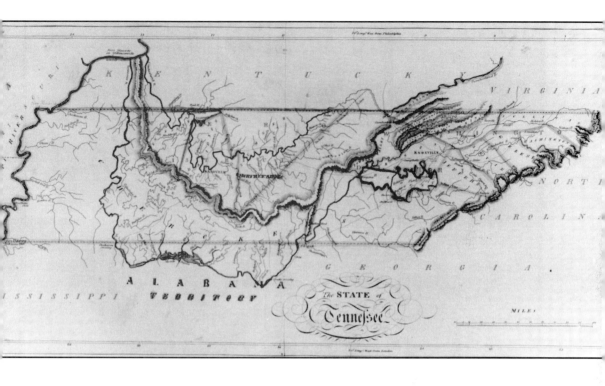

A map of Tennessee after it
gained statehood in 1796.
One of its eastern counties was
named "Sevier."

that met in the newly formed city of Knoxville in
January 1796. In June of that year, Tennessee
became the 16th state of the Union.

During these years, Sevier largely stayed out of
the public eye. He did lead several raids against the
Cherokee Indians, who continued waging sporadic
war against the settlers who had invaded their land.
In 1797, Sevier came back into prominence when
he was elected the first governor of Tennessee. He
served six terms, from 1796 to 1801 and from 1803
to 1809. After leaving the governor's office, he was
elected to the state Senate for one two-year term.
Then, in 1811, Sevier was elected to represent the
state of Tennessee in the United States House of

Representatives, where he served for the rest of his life.

Though John Sevier was involved in public service during all those years, he spent most of his time as a gentleman farmer, overseeing the slaves who worked the fields of his large farm not far from Knoxville. He was, in addition, a trustee of both Washington College and Blount College (later the University of Tennessee). Family matters also occupied much of his time. He and Kate hosted teas, played cards with other government officials and their wives, and frequently attended church together. Sevier, the one-time Indian fighter, rebel, and pioneer, became a pillar of frontier society.

In 1815, Sevier was named to serve on a commission that would survey lands ceded to the U.S. government by the Creek Indians. While in Alabama on that mission, John Sevier died at the age of 70. Originally buried at Fort Decatur on the Tallapoosa River in central Alabama, his remains were eventually removed to Knoxville. The epitaph on his headstone recognized his many accomplishments: "John Sevier . . . pioneer, soldier, statesman, and one of the founders of the Republic; Governor of the State of Franklin; six terms Governor of Tennessee; four times elected to Congress; the typical pioneer who conquered the wilderness and fashioned the State; a projector and hero of King's Mountain; thirty-five battles, thirty-five victories; his Indian war-cry, 'Here they are! Come on boys, come on!'"

Tennessee from Statehood to the Civil War

After gaining statehood in 1796, Tennessee thrived. In 1819, the first steamboat reached Nashville on the Cumberland River, promising a healthy new stream of traffic and trade along the state's many waterways. The city of Memphis, which would become a center of the cotton industry, was planned and settled in the same year. Immigrants continued to arrive in the growing state, especially after the Cherokee and Chickasaw Indians of the region were moved farther west in the late 1830s.

Tennessee rapidly established a tradition of providing heroes to the emerging United States. In addition to John Sevier, famous Tennesseans include Andrew Jackson, the commanding general in the Battle of New Orleans during the War of 1812 and later president of the United States; Davy Crockett, who died in defense of the Alamo in Texas; and General Sam Houston, who eventually became the first president of the Republic of Texas. In fact, so many Tennesseans flocked to fight in the Mexican War (1846-1848) that Tennessee became known as "the volunteer state."

During the Civil War, Tennessee was divided, with most residents of the eastern part of the state supporting the Union and most of those living in west and central Tennessee supporting the Confederacy.

Because of this division, Tennessee was the last state to secede from the Union. As a border state important to both sides, it was the site of many battles during the conflict between the North and the South, including the bloody Battle of Shiloh, in which thousands lost their lives. More battles were fought on Tennessee land than in any state except Virginia.

One of America's most famous frontiersmen, David Crockett (1786-1836) spent most of his youth in the Tennessee woods before gaining a reputation as an Indian fighter, a politician, and a hero of the Texan struggle against Mexican rule.

Chapter Five

Stephen Austin
and the
Colonization of Texas

*I*n June 1821, 27-year-old Stephen Austin was in New Orleans studying law and working as a journalist when he received a letter from his mother. She wrote that Stephen's father was near death at the family's home in Arkansas and that he wanted Stephen to "take his place . . . to go on with the business in the same way he would have done."

The "business" of which Stephen's mother spoke was the establishment of an American settlement in what was then the Mexican province of Texas. In response to that letter, Stephen Austin quickly left New Orleans, taking the first step in the process that would earn him the name "The Father of Texas" and recognition as one of America's greatest pioneer settlers.

"I have spent the prime of my life and worn out my constitution [health] in trying to colonize this country," Stephen Austin (1793-1836) said of Texas. "It has assumed the character of a religion, for the guidance of my thoughts and actions, for fifteen years."

Stephen Austin was born on November 3, 1793, in Wythe County on the southwestern frontier of Virginia, the eldest of four children of Moses and Maria Austin. When Stephen was three, the family moved to present-day Missouri (then known as Upper Louisiana) after Moses Austin's business in Virginia failed. In his new home, Moses operated a successful lead mine.

In 1804, at the age of 11, Stephen was sent to Colchester, Connecticut, where he enrolled in the Bacon Academy, a prestigious preparatory school. Following four years of study at Bacon, Stephen attended Transylvania University in Lexington, Kentucky. In April 1810, at the age of 16, he received a certificate showing that he had completed his studies at Transylvania. That certificate stated that he "conducted himself in an exemplary and praiseworthy manner" during his time at the university. This is hardly surprising, for Stephen was described throughout his life as intelligent, thoughtful, gentle, and charming.

For the next several years, Stephen helped his father in his various businesses. Then, in 1814, the U.S. Congress made Upper Louisiana into the Missouri Territory, and Stephen was elected to serve in the territorial legislature. He was 21 years old.

In 1819, before his full term in the legislature ended, Stephen, with his parents, migrated into the new territory of Arkansas in search of greater opportunity. In July 1820, at the age of 26, Stephen was appointed a judge of the first judicial district in Arkansas. Although he accepted the appointment,

Stephen seemed hesitant about his career path. By August, he was living in New Orleans, studying law and working as a newspaper editor for the *Louisiana Advertiser*.

While Stephen was working in New Orleans, his father, Moses, traveled to Texas to investigate the possibility of trade with the region. There, in late 1820, he submitted a petition to the Spanish government of Mexico, asking for permission to settle 300 Anglo-American families in the area. Moses's petition was granted because he had once been a Spanish citizen, having lived in Missouri while it was Spanish territory. He started for home but fell ill during his journey, and on June 10, 1821, he died.

On his deathbed, Moses Austin (1761-1821) thought only of his plans to colonize Texas. As Maria Austin wrote in a letter to their son Stephen, "He called me to his bedside and with much distress and difficulty of speech beged [sic] me to tell you to take his place and if God in his wisdom thought best to disappoint him in the accomplishment of his wishes and plans . . . he prayed him to extend his goodness to you and enable you to go on with the business in the same way he would have done."

Texas before Austin

The first Europeans to see the area we know as Texas were Spanish explorers, including Alonso Álvarez de Piñeda in 1519, Álvar Nuñez Cabeza de Vaca about 10 years later, and Francisco Vásquez de Coronado in 1541. Other expeditions followed, and, in 1682, the Spanish established the first European settlement in Texas, a mission called Corpus Christi de Isleta (or Ysleta), near the present-day city of El Paso.

Three years later, the great French explorer Robert de La Salle set up an outpost called Fort St. Louis on the Gulf Coast of Texas. La Salle, however, came to the region purely by accident, having gotten lost while searching for the mouth of the Mississippi River. Shipwrecked on the Texas coast, he was killed by his own men. The fort that he established was eventually destroyed by Indians, and its occupants died from disease.

Anxious to settle Texas, the Spanish sent more than 100 expeditions to the area from Mexico during the first half of the eighteenth century. Other missions were built—including one at San Antonio, which became the major Spanish settlement in Texas. By 1750, Texas was firmly under Spanish control.

Early in the next century, as United States citizens living in the East began looking for new land, American interest in Texas increased. Several times in the early 1800s, Americans led ill-fated expeditions into Texas in attempts to wrest the territory from Spain. Finally, in 1820, a colonist named Moses Austin visited Texas and obtained permission to settle Americans there.

Following his father's death, Stephen moved quickly to make Moses Austin's plans for a Texas settlement a reality. By mid-July, he was in San Antonio, the headquarters for the government of the Mexican state of Coahuila-Texas. There he met with the provincial governor, Antonio de Martinez, and obtained his approval to go ahead with the settlement.

After receiving the governor's approval, Stephen Austin searched for the ideal location for a colony and found it in east Texas, between the Lavaca and Brazos Rivers. His plans were reported in newspapers in the United States, and his proposed colony quickly attracted many settlers. He was soon convinced he could settle 1,500 families in his colony as easily as 300.

Mexico, at that time, was in a state of political turmoil. It had been a colony of Spain until early 1821, when it declared its independence. A Mexican national government had replaced the Spanish colonial government, and, in a major setback for Austin's plans, this new government reversed Antonio de Martinez's decision about the proposed colony in Texas. Governor Martinez, who wanted the eastern part of Texas settled, urged Austin to go to the capital of Mexico, Mexico City, to argue his case.

Austin arrived in Mexico City in April 1822, and for the next year, he pleaded, petitioned, and pestered the Mexican government to give its approval to his plan. Time and again, his hopes were dashed. Even in the face of these difficulties, however, he presented an optimistic view to about 50 settlers who were already in his proposed colony. In a letter written in July 1822, he told the colonists "not to be discouraged at the gloomy prospect which wild woods present to them on their first arrival, [for] a short time will change the scene, and we shall enjoy many a merry dance and wedding frolic together."

Austin made an extensive tour of Texas while looking for a place to settle, traveling through the equivalent of 23 modern-day counties. He described the area as "an entire wilderness from the Sabine to the San Antonio River. Its civilized population was comprised of the towns of Bexar [San Antonio] and Bahía [Goliad] and did not exceed 2,500 souls. The whole country was filled with hostile and pilfering Indians."

Austin arrived in Mexico City, he later said, "without acquaintances, without friends . . . with barely the means of paying my expenses for a few months . . . destitute of almost everything necessary to insure success in such a mission as I had undertaken but the integrity of my intentions." Mexico, he added, was in "an unsettled state . . . almost sinking under its efforts to preserve the public peace and order."

Finally, in January 1823, Austin's petition was approved. He was granted a huge slice of southeastern Texas running from the Gulf of Mexico to a line between the present-day cities of San Antonio and Bastrop. Austin was given permission to bring settlers into the area, which included some of the most fertile land in the entire province.

Austin was a busy man as he worked to guarantee the prosperity of the colony and of its settlers. He established border settlements and occasionally used force to keep Native Americans out of his colony.

A topographic map of southeastern Texas by Stephen Austin, probably made in 1822

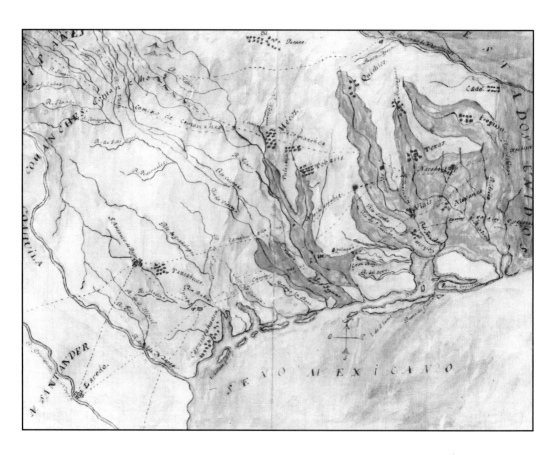

The Native Americans of Texas

Long before Europeans set foot in the lands that eventually became the state of Texas, the region was home to prehistoric peoples who gradually evolved into the various tribes we know as Native Americans.

When the first Spanish explorers came to Texas in the early sixteenth century, two major Indian tribal groups lived in the region: the Apache and the Caddo. The Apache were fierce warriors who tried to resist the Spanish invasion of their lands and, later, the settlement of Texas by immigrants from the United States. Unable to stop the loss of their homes and lands, the Apache were eventually forced onto reservations in New Mexico and Arizona.

Caddo is the name given to a group of tribes whose earliest homeland was the Red River valley in what is now northeastern Texas. Like the Apache, the Caddo lived by hunting and farming. For the most part, they had peaceful relations with European settlers, but contact with the settlers eventually led to a disintegration of the Caddo culture and a sharp decline in the group's population, from about 8,000 in the early seventeenth century to about 500 in 1880.

A third Indian group posed the greatest threat to European settlement of Texas. These were the Comanche, nomadic people who came from the north and began hunting and establishing villages in Texas in the early eighteenth century. Excellent horsemen and brave warriors, they fiercely resisted white settlement of their lands and made their territory unsafe for settlers for more than a century. During the late nineteenth century, however, the Comanche were defeated and, like other Native American peoples, removed to reservations.

A Comanche chief named Asa-to-Yet poses with a gun in about 1870.

Until the colonists elected their own officials, Austin was the supreme military, judicial, and civil officer in his colony. He had absolute authority either to allow settlers into the colony or to keep them out. He made it plain to those who crossed into Texas that he believed their success and the success of the colony depended on their willingness to follow his lead. They had nothing to fear from him, he said, since all he desired was their prosperity. "In fact," he once said, "I look upon them [the settlers] as one great family who are under my care."

Austin mapped the lands under his control and explored the coastline. He also took care of all the business associated with getting land titles issued to colonists. As the colony's lawgiver, he wrote civil and criminal codes and served as a judge and mediator. Austin often provided even more personal aid to settlers. More than once, he was asked by worried parents in the United States to watch over sons and daughters who had settled in Texas. Frequently, new colonists expected him to purchase needed goods for them, advancing them money until crops came in.

Of course, Austin was rewarded for his labors. He received large land grants from Mexico: over 65,000 acres of land for every 200 families settled. In addition, settlers were supposed to pay him twelve and a half cents per acre for land they received. As early as 1824, however, many of the first colonists complained about having to pay Austin for lands that were given to him free of charge by the Mexican government. In response, Austin told the colonists that because of expenses involved in settling the 300 families authorized under his original contract with the Mexican government, he had incurred a debt of $77,600.50. If all the settlers paid what they owed him, he would collect $166,500. But, Austin noted, that debt was "payable in property at a distant period and in small installments."

We do not know how much of the money Austin collected, but some of the settlers' debts were never settled. Most of the payments that were made were in the form of horses, cattle, or produce. Austin later said that this property was sold for just half or one-third of what was actually due him. The money issue was finally resolved in 1825, when the Mexican government enacted a new national colonization law that gave Austin the legal right to collect money from settlers. This law permitted him and other immigration agents, known as *empresarios*, to take out contracts with the Mexican government to bring new settlers to Texas. In exchange, the *empresarios*

Austin's grant from the Mexican government instructed him to allot to the head of each family a *labor* of land (177 acres) for farming and 74 *labor*s for ranching, for a total of one *sitio*, or square league. The grant also gave Austin the right to found a town and dispose of lots within that town. In July 1824, he established the town of San Felipe de Austin on the banks of the Brazos River.

"The colonists . . . say that I ought to do everything for them free, because the government has already paid me in the lands that came to me as *empresario*. But they do not reflect that I can not live on lands; that I can not eat them, make clothes of them, nor sell them; and that I have spent all that I had in their service."
—Stephen Austin

received generous land grants, plus fees from the settlers.

The Texas colonies had no difficulty attracting settlers. The United States was still reeling from the financial crash of 1819, and many people were seeking land that they could farm. Public land in the United States cost $1.25 per acre, or $200 for 160 acres of what was often some of the worst land available. In Texas, a family could purchase 4,428 acres for $30, payable in installments.

Austin issues land titles to eager new colonists.

Austin was the most successful of all the Texas *empresarios*. His colony attracted settlers by the hundreds. By the fall of 1825, about 2,000 people had settled in the new colony. Most lived between the Colorado and Brazos Rivers (in the coastal area south of present-day Houston) or farther west along the Gulf Coast, between the San Antonio and Lavaca Rivers (southeast of the city of San Antonio). Austin expanded his contract with the government three times in the next four years, allowing him to settle nearly 900 more families in his colony.

During the Austin colony's earliest years, immigration to Texas was slowed because of Mexico's hostility to slavery. Slavery, it must be remembered, was legal and widely practiced in the United States in those years. Austin knew that many would-be colonists would not come to Texas if they could not own slaves.

During the years from 1823 to 1828, largely because he wanted to see his colony grow and prosper, Austin supported slavery. In those years, he wrote several petitions to the Mexican authorities urging them to recognize formally the right of immigrants to own slaves. In May 1828, the authorities did just that. They passed a law that, in effect, enabled immigrants to free their slaves and then immediately make them indentured servants for life.

About 1830, Austin had a change of heart, probably because he heard of slave revolts in Virginia and other southern states. He began a quiet anti-slavery campaign hoping to end the practice in Texas. Soon, though, immigrants—including those from

"In the beginning of this settlement I was compelled to hold out the idea that slavery would be tolerated, and I succeeded in getting it tolerated for a time. . . . I did this to get a start, for otherwise it would have been next to impossible to have started at all. . . . Slavery is now most positively prohibited by our Constitution and by a number of Laws, and I do hope it may always be so."
—Stephen Austin

states where slavery was outlawed—made it clear that they favored slavery in Texas. Austin dropped his antislavery campaign.

The issue of religious freedom also troubled many would-be colonists of Texas. Roman Catholicism was the state religion of Mexico, and while settlers in Texas were not forced to become Catholics, they were deprived of Protestant ministers and churches. In 1834, this issue was resolved when the Mexican government passed a law that declared, "No person shall be molested for political and religious opinions, provided he shall not disturb the public order."

With the restrictions against slavery and religious freedom removed, the population of Austin's colony increased even more rapidly. Immigrants knew that they would have the best chances of finding success in his settlements. Unlike some of the *empresarios*, who were little more than greedy land speculators, Austin was honest and knew how to get along with the Mexican government. His colony was large enough to protect itself from Native American attacks. And those who were familiar with Texas knew that his territories offered a mild climate, abundant rainfall, the best lands for farming and ranching, the timber needed for building, and easy access to the Gulf of Mexico. The population of Austin's settlements stood at 2,021 persons in 1825; 4,248 in 1831; and 5,660 a year later.

The Mexican government had wanted Texas to be settled by Anglo-Americans both to increase trade with the United States and to protect Mexico from the Indians of the area. Many in the government, however, became concerned about the rising number of settlers in the new colonies. They were also concerned when Andrew Jackson became president of the United States in 1829. Jackson made no secret of his desire to gain new territories in the Southwest, and many in Mexico believed he might use force to make Texas part of the United States.

On April 6, 1830, Mexico responded by passing a law forbidding further immigration to Texas by Americans. The law had other provisions. It called for the military occupation of Texas by Mexican troops, settlement in the province by Swiss and German immigrants as well as people from other parts of Mexico, and increased trade between Texas and the rest of Mexico.

Because they were viewed as loyal to the government of Mexico and because their colonies were successful, Austin and fellow *empresario* Green De Witt were exempted from the new law. They were allowed to continue expanding their settlements. Hundreds of other Americans scattered throughout Texas, however, did not support Mexican rule and were ready to rebel. Hundreds more who were not residents of the area believed that Texas should be a territory of the United States. They were waiting just outside Texas's borders, ready to fight if they were called.

After passage of the 1830 law, Austin hoped that a permanent and peaceful solution to the differences between the Anglo-American colonists and the Mexican authorities would be reached. During the next several years, however, dissatisfaction among the settlers grew. Many outside the Austin and De Witt camps pushed for the repeal of the law of April 1830. They also demanded a repeal of antislavery regulations and the establishment of a separate state government for Texas, then a part of the Mexican state of Coahuila-Texas.

The discord in Texas came to a head in 1833. On April 1 of that year, the same day that General Antonio López de Santa Anna was sworn in as the new president of Mexico, delegates from around Texas met at a convention at San Felipe de Austin. At that convention, a proposed constitution was framed for the Mexican state of Texas, and Austin was chosen to present a list of grievances to Santa Anna. He left Texas for Mexico City on June 1.

At first, things went well for Austin in the Mexican capital. Santa Anna was out of town, and Austin met with his vice president, Valentín Gomez Farías. Gomez Farías was willing to approve the repeal of the immigration restrictions of 1830 and at least to discuss the possibility of Mexican statehood for Texas. Austin left Mexico City in a hopeful mood.

Very soon after his departure, however, sentiment in the Mexican capital changed, and Austin was overtaken by Mexican troops who arrested him on charges of treason. For the next year and a half, he was kept in jail or under house arrest in Mexico City before being granted his freedom by Santa Anna. He returned to Texas on September 1, 1835.

Back in Texas, Austin argued in favor of trying to find a peaceful solution to the continuing conflict

Austin was afraid that the news of his arrest in Mexico would lead to an uprising against the Mexican authorities in Texas. He wrote several letters urging calm, including one to a friend in which he said: "I hope there will be no excitement about my arrest. All I can be accused of is that I have labored arduously, faithfully, and perhaps at particular moments . . . with more impatience and irritation than I ought to have shown, to have Texas made a state of the Mexican Confederation. . . . This is all, and this is no crime."

between the Texans and the Mexican government. Even as he urged peace, however, Santa Anna was dispatching troops to the province on the pretext that Texas was already in rebellion. Austin had long preached loyalty to Mexico, but on September 19, less than three weeks after his return from Mexico City, he issued a statement that said, "war is our only recourse."

Fighting erupted on October 2, in a battle on the Gonzales River during which Texans fought Mexican troops for the possession of a single cannon.

Although Austin described Mexico City as "magnificent" on his 1822 visit, during his 18-month imprisonment he received a different impression. For a time, Austin endured solitary confinement in a windowless 13-by-16-foot cell, with only a few books and a diary to keep him occupied while the government continued to delay his case in court.

Troops in the field that day elected Austin commander-in-chief. By mid-October, Austin, with a force of about 600 men, was laying siege to the provincial capital of San Antonio. The army fighting for Texas was a ragtag group made up of adventurers and volunteers from southern states, including such famous figures as Jim Bowie and Davy Crockett. The Texas forces were brave but disorganized, and Austin, with no military experience, was not the best man to lead them. The attempt to take San Antonio soon failed.

In early November, while the Texas troops were still camped outside San Antonio, Austin and fellow Texan Sam Houston traveled to San Felipe de Austin to attend another meeting of Texas delegates. At that meeting, Austin was chosen to go to Washington, D.C., to enlist the aid of the U.S. government for the freedom fighters in Texas. He was

James Bowie (1795-1836) was a Tennessee frontiersman who settled in Texas in 1828. He became a naturalized Mexican citizen, joined the Texas fight for freedom in 1835, and was killed in the heroic defense at the Alamo. He is best known for designing the Bowie knife, a hunting knife with a 9-to-15-inch single-edged blade that became notorious as a fighting weapon on the frontier.

in Washington when the Battle of the Alamo, one of the most famous battles in American history, took place. Santa Anna and his army captured the Alamo and killed all its defenders, but on April 20, 1836, the Texans, under the command of Sam Houston, defeated the Mexicans in the Battle of San Jacinto. Texas had won its independence.

On September 5, 1836, the new Republic of Texas elected a president. In that election, Austin was defeated by the immensely popular Houston.

The Texan army won the Battle of San Jacinto after just 20 minutes of fighting, but violence against the defeated Mexicans continued for several hours afterward.

General Antonio López de Santa Anna

Antonio López de Santa Anna, the Mexican general who fought the Texan rebels, had a long and turbulent career in the political life of Mexico. Born in 1794, Santa Anna joined the army as a teenager. He helped Mexico gain its freedom from Spain in 1821 and later led the armies that ended Spanish attempts to reclaim Mexico. In 1833, he was elected president, but chose instead to overthrow the government and establish himself as dictator. Santa Anna commanded the victorious Mexican army at the Alamo in 1836, but later that year he was defeated at the Battle of San Jacinto.

After Santa Anna returned to Mexico, he was removed from power and forced into retirement. In 1838, he appeared on the scene again when he led the Mexican forces that repulsed a French attack on the city of Veracruz. After losing a leg in the fighting, Santa Anna was hailed as a hero, and by 1841, he was ruling Mexico as president with the powers of a dictator. Overthrown in 1845, he was recalled the following year to lead the army against the United States in the Mexican War. Following the defeat of Mexico in 1847, Santa Anna fled to Jamaica, but in 1853 he was again recalled and once more established himself as a dictator. Two years later, the people of Mexico, tired of his harsh treatment, removed him from office. At that time, he fled once again to the Caribbean, where he lived as an exile until he returned to Mexico in 1874. Santa Anna died in Mexico City in 1876, old and penniless.

Houston quickly named Austin his secretary of state, but three months later, tired and weak from his 20 years of service to Texas, Austin died. He was just 43 years old. After all his hard work helping to found what would become the state of Texas, he was land-rich but cash-poor. His home in San Felipe de Austin had been burned during the conflict with Mexico. Austin's deathbed was a pallet on the floor of a two-room clapboard shack.

Stephen Austin had never married. Texas was his wife and family. A letter he wrote not long before his death provided him with a fitting epitaph. "I am nothing more than an individual citizen of this country, but I feel a more lively interest for its welfare than can be expressed," he said. "The prosperity of Texas has been the object of my labors, the idol of my existence."

As Austin lay dying, he dreamed that Texas's independence had been acknowledged by the United States (something that did not actually happen until 1837). His last words were, "Texas recognized. . . . Did you see it in the papers?"

In 1839, Mirabeau Lamar, the second president of Texas, chose a small settlement called Waterloo to be the republic's new capital. The town grew quickly, and it was renamed Austin in honor of Texas's original settler.

Chapter Six

Sam Houston
and the
Fight for Texas

Near sunset on July 26, 1863, a 70-year-old man named Sam Houston lay in bed at his home in the Texas town of Huntsville. Sick with pneumonia, he struggled to draw breath as Margaret, his wife of many years, read to him from the Bible. Suddenly, he began to toss and turn. Margaret rushed to kneel by his bed. She took his hand in hers.

"Texas. Texas. . . ," he said. And then he died.

It was fitting that Houston's last thoughts should be of Texas. During much of his life, he had dedicated all his energies to what we know as the Lone Star State. He had served it as a general during the Texas rebellion against Mexico, as the first president of the Republic of Texas, and as a senator representing the state of Texas in the U.S. Congress.

With a life as colorful as the bright checkered shirts he always wore, Samuel Houston (1793-1863) guided Texas from independence to statehood and became its most honored hero.

In those roles, he became one of America's most famous pioneer statesmen and leaders.

Samuel Houston was born on March 2, 1793, near the town of Lexington in central Virginia. He was the fifth son born to Major Sam Houston—a veteran of the Revolutionary War who remained in the army after the war ended—and his wife, Elizabeth. Elizabeth Paxton Houston, the daughter of a wealthy farmer, was, by all accounts, a remarkable woman. She was intelligent, strong-willed, and resourceful, all traits she passed on to her son Sam.

While Sam was growing up, his father was often away from home on army business. His mother ran the family's fairly substantial farm with the help of about six slaves. While Sam also did some work in the fields, he had little interest in farming. He spent much of his time hunting, fishing in nearby creeks, and roaming the woods that surrounded the Houston farm. At about the age of eight, he began his formal education in what was known as a "field school." There, he learned to read and write and do some basic arithmetic. Most of his education, however—particularly in history and geography—he received at home, from his mother.

Sometime in 1807 (the exact date is uncertain), Sam's father died while away from home inspecting a military post. Late that same year or early in 1808, Elizabeth Houston sold the family farm in Virginia and purchased property near the little town of Maryville in east Tennessee, where she had relatives and friends. Soon, the Houstons—15-year-old Sam, his mother, his four older brothers, and a boy and three girls born after Sam, along with two female slaves and their children—moved to their new home. The Houston house in Tennessee was, at first, a simple one-room log cabin. Over time, it would be expanded into a comfortable and well-furnished two-story home.

After the move to Tennessee, young Sam at first divided his time between working in the family's fields and attending classes at a small rural school, where he probably attained the equivalent of a third- or fourth-grade education. At the age of 16, however, Sam walked away from the classroom, never to reenter it as a student.

Not long after ending his formal schooling, Sam started working as a clerk in a nearby village dry-goods store. It didn't take him long to discover he wasn't suited for clerking. A rebellious young man, he ran away from his job and his family, taking to the woods he loved.

At that time, a band of about 300 Cherokee Indians lived on Hiwassee Island, located around 90 miles southwest of Maryville at a spot where the Tennessee and Hiwassee Rivers meet. Somehow, Sam made his way to that island and became a member of the Cherokee band, which was led by Chief Ooleteka (called John Jolly by the settlers). For the next three years, Sam lived with the Cherokee. He learned their language and their ways of hunting and fishing. More important, he learned to respect the Native Americans and to feel sympathy for them as they saw their ancient way of life disappearing.

While at the Maryville school, Sam read an English translation of Homer's famous epic poem *The Iliad*, which he loved. He claimed that he left school because his teacher refused to teach him Latin and Greek so that he could read the classical epics in their original languages.

The Cherokee

The Cherokee tribe was an important Native American group in the south-central region during the period of European settlement. Originally dwelling in the Great Lakes area, the Cherokee migrated to present-day North and South Carolina, Tennessee, and northern Georgia and Alabama before the first Europeans came to the New World. They lived in small towns and villages, each settlement governed by a chief and a council made up of warriors and other important people in the community. Like other Native American peoples, however, the Cherokee were devastated by illness following their first contact with Europeans. Smallpox and other diseases ravaged their towns, and by the 1760s, the Cherokee population had been reduced to half its original size.

During the long period when France and England struggled for dominance in the New World, the Cherokee were often allies of the British. They also supported the British during the Revolutionary War. After the war, conflict continued between the United States and the Cherokee until 1791, when the tribe ceded some of their lands to the U.S. government.

Faced with the loss of their homeland, many Cherokee made an effort to adopt the European-American way of life. In 1820, the tribe established a system of government modeled on that of the United States. Tribal leaders, including a principal chief, senators, and representatives similar to congressmen, were elected. In 1827, the Cherokee drafted a constitution and created the Cherokee Nation.

If the Cherokee people hoped that their actions would win them lasting friends among the settlers, they were disappointed. After the discovery of gold on Cherokee land in Georgia in 1829, fair play was forgotten as the Indians were gradually forced from their now-valuable territory. In 1830, the U.S. Congress passed the Indian Removal Act, which allowed the federal government to renegotiate existing Indian treaties, forcing tribes to give up their lands in the East in exchange for new homes west of the Mississippi River. In 1832, the Cherokee attempted to maintain control over their territory in Georgia by bringing a case to the U.S. Supreme Court. The Court ruled in favor of the Cherokee, but the state of Georgia, as well as President Andrew Jackson and other federal officials, simply disregarded the court's decision.

In 1835, three years after the court ruling, about 500 of the tribe's leaders signed a treaty agreeing to trade Cherokee land in the southeast for land in the Indian Territory (now Oklahoma), plus a payment of $5,700,000. Most members of the tribe weren't consulted before the agreement was reached, and they refused to accept it, but their resistance was in vain. In 1838, the federal government began forcibly moving the Cherokee from their lands. While about 1,000 members of the tribe escaped into the mountains of North Carolina, most of the Cherokee—about 17,000 men, women, and children—were herded west in a forced march known as the "Trail of Tears," in which about 4,000 Cherokee died.

Once settled in the Indian Territory, the Cherokee started new lives, building schools and establishing farms and businesses. It would not be long, however, before their lives were again disrupted and their lands taken as settlers invaded the Indian Territory.

Despite all their hardships, the Cherokee people have survived to become the largest Native American tribe in the United States. There are currently more than 350,000 Cherokee living in the U.S.

The Trail of Tears, as depicted in a 1939 mural by Elizabeth Janes

Chief Ooleteka advanced to
become chief of the
Cherokee Nation in 1820.

During his time with the Cherokee, Sam, now a tall, strong young man, was adopted by Ooleteka and given the Indian name Kalanu ("The Raven"). Perhaps, in the Cherokee leader, Sam found a father figure to replace his own dead father. In any event, he must have felt truly welcome in the Indian community, for while he lived on Hiwassee Island, he returned home to visit his family only a few times.

At the age of 19, Sam Houston learned that both his younger sister Isabella and his older brother Paxton had died. He realized that the time had come for him to go home to help his mother. Sometime in 1812, he left the Hiwassee camp and returned to Maryville.

Sam Houston in Cherokee dress, which he continued to wear often throughout his life.

Following his return, Houston spent about six months working as a teacher in a one-room school not far from the family farm. In those days, being a teacher did not require the years of education it does today. It was enough that Houston knew the basics of reading, writing, and arithmetic, along with some simple geography. He soon had a large number of students, including some middle-aged men. Each student paid Houston eight dollars per year for his or her education; one-third of this sum was payable in cash, one-third in corn, and one-third in cotton cloth.

While Houston later said he enjoyed his time as a teacher, he stuck with his new job for only about six months before the promise of adventure called him again. At that time, in late 1812, the United States was at war with Great Britain. Houston, then 20 years of age, volunteered for service, entering the army in early 1813.

Commissioned as an ensign and soon promoted to third lieutenant, Houston fought in the Battle of Horseshoe Bend, Alabama, on March 28, 1814. Under the command of General Andrew Jackson, the American troops defeated a group of Creek Indians who were fighting as allies of the British. Houston fought bravely, but was badly wounded by an arrow in the thigh and a gunshot in the right shoulder. His heroism impressed Jackson, who would later become Houston's friend, political patron, and adviser.

Houston remained in the army when the war ended, and in 1817 Jackson sent him to persuade the Cherokee of Hiwassee Island to give up their

In 1812, the United States declared war on Great Britain—partly to stop British interference with its ships at sea, but also because American settlers were moving into lands in the West claimed by the British and their Indian allies. During the war, Britain won several major victories and even invaded Washington, D.C., setting fire to the White House. In late 1814, following victories by the Americans during battles at Pittsburgh, Pennsylvania, and at Fort McHenry, Maryland, the British agreed to negotiate. The war finally came to an end on December 24, 1814, with the signing of a treaty. Costly to both sides in terms of lives and property, the War of 1812 had no clear winner.

After being shot in the thigh at the Battle of Horseshoe Bend, Houston ordered one of his men to pull the arrow out of his leg, but twice, the man failed to free it. Waving his sword, Houston ordered his subordinate, "Try again and, if you fail this time, I will smite you to the earth." The arrow came out, but it left Houston with a permanent limp.

In the early nineteenth century, lawyers, like teachers, did not receive the long training required today. All that was needed was a term—usually two or three years—working with a practicing lawyer.

lands and move to the territory that is now Arkansas. Houston did so, firmly believing that his Native American friends could live undisturbed in the West. He fought to win the best treatment possible for the Cherokee, but finally resigned his military commission in early 1818, disgusted with national politics. Houston went back to Tennessee and began studying to become a lawyer.

From the beginning of his career outside the army, Houston was a success. By all accounts, he was one of the most popular figures—and successful lawyers—in eastern Tennessee in his day. He had characteristics that made frontier men and women alike look up to him and trust him. Houston was an impressive speaker, able to sway audiences with the power of his words. He also made an impressive appearance; tall (about six feet, two inches), with keen gray eyes and long hair worn in a Native American style, he dressed dramatically in colorful shirts.

His personal popularity soon convinced Houston he should seek public office. In 1820, he was elected district attorney for Davidson county (of which Nashville was the county seat). With Andrew Jackson's encouragement and support, he was elected to the U.S. Congress three years later, gaining reelection in 1825. In 1827, Houston became the sixth governor of Tennessee. Then, in early 1829, while Houston was campaigning for reelection as governor, his life took an unexpected and still unexplained turn.

At that time, Houston married Eliza Allen, the daughter of a wealthy and influential Nashville family. Something—we're not sure what—happened shortly after the wedding, causing Eliza to leave her husband of just a few months, return to her father's house, and refuse to have any more to do with Houston. The breakup of the marriage was a public scandal that ruined Houston's political career in Tennessee. Deeply depressed, he immediately resigned as governor and left for the Indian country to the west.

By the end of 1829, Houston was firmly established at a trading post called the Wigwam, located on the Neosha River in what is now northeastern

Oklahoma. Here he lived among Cherokee people who had been forced from the lands they had been promised in Arkansas. Among them were some of Houston's old friends from Hiwassee Island—Chief Ooleteka and his family, including his niece, Tiana Rogers Gentry. Houston had first met Tiana when he lived with Ooleteka's band at Hiwassee. She had later married a white blacksmith, David Gentry, and was now a widow. In 1830, Houston and Tiana were married in a traditional Cherokee ceremony, although the couple would spend very little time together in the following years.

By this time, Houston was drinking heavily even by the standards of the frontier, where drinking was commonplace. His consumption of alcohol, however, never seemed to interfere with his work for the Indians, which included annual trips to Washington to plead for more humane and fair treatment for his Native American friends.

During this period of his life, Houston first began to become involved in the affairs of Texas, which was then part of the Mexican state of Coahuila. As early as 1829, old friends who had settled in Texas invited him to join them there. In 1832, Houston made a journey to Texas, apparently as an agent of President Andrew Jackson, his old friend and commander from the War of 1812. Houston's purpose was to find out how many Indians lived in the eastern part of the region, how much of a threat they would be to settlers from the United States, and if they might be willing to make peace. Among the tribes he met on this fact-finding mission

Like Houston, Andrew Jackson (1767-1845) began his career as a lawyer in Tennessee and then became the state's representative in the U.S. Congress. After serving in several more political posts, Jackson became a national hero in the War of 1812. His immense popularity helped him win the presidency in 1828.

were the Comanche Indians who lived around San Antonio and a branch of the eastern Cherokee who had migrated to Texas.

Houston requested and received a land grant in Stephen Austin's colony, and in the following year he attended a convention in the colony's major city, San Felipe de Austin. There, Stephen Austin was given the task of persuading officials in Mexico to make Texas a separate Mexican state. Houston helped to write Texas's new constitution, but his interest in Texas was still secondary to his life with the Native Americans.

Although Texas remained a part of Mexico, by the 1830s its population was largely American. Many of these settlers had little respect for the current Mexican government and looked forward to a time when Texas would be part of the United States. In an attempt to slow or stop American immigration, Mexican dictator Antonio López de Santa Anna abolished slavery in the state and enforced the collection of taxes. The Americans living in Texas immediately rose up in arms in what is known as the Texas Rebellion. Fighting began in late 1835 at the Battle of Gonzales, about 50 miles east of San Antonio, where the Mexican forces were defeated.

By the time the rebellion began, Houston had left the Wigwam for good and was living in Nacogdoches, Texas, where he practiced law. As an army veteran and former U.S. congressman, he was an important man in the community. Even before the first shots of the Texas Rebellion were fired, he was made commander of a group of Texas soldiers recruited in Nacogdoches. Stephen Austin was the overall commander of the Texas army, which was made up mainly of volunteers, many of them newcomers to Texas from Tennessee and Kentucky.

In late 1835, while Austin and his volunteers were chasing the Mexican army from Gonzales toward San Antonio, the leaders of the Texas rebels met in San Felipe de Austin. They established a provisional government, which quickly decided that Austin and two other men should go to Washington to seek financial and political help from the United

During the days leading up to the Texas Rebellion and even after the fighting had begun, Houston hoped that President Andrew Jackson would find a way to settle the conflict between the Texans and Mexicans. He wanted the president to purchase Texas and annex it as part of the United States. Houston was a realist, however, and he knew that such an outcome was unlikely. In a letter to a friend, he wrote, "War in defense of our rights, our oaths, and our constitutions is inevitable, in Texas! . . . Our war cry is 'Liberty or death.'"

States. The government then named Sam Houston the commander of the Texas army.

While Houston was still building his army, the nature of the war changed with a battle that became famous in American history. On February 23, 1836, a Mexican army of more than 2,000 men commanded by Santa Anna reached the outskirts of San Antonio. Inside the city, which had been captured about three months earlier by Texan volunteers, a

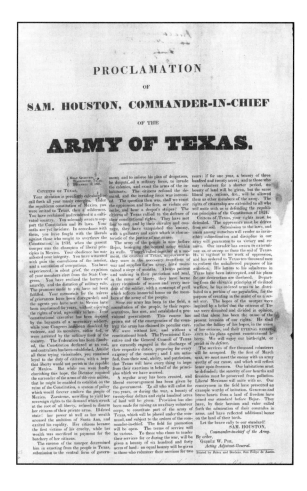

On December 12, 1835, Houston issued a call for 5,000 volunteers to fight in the Texan army. Its final line was "Let the brave rally to our standard!"

In defending the Alamo, Colonel Travis and his co-commander, Jim Bowie, disobeyed direct orders from Houston, who had instructed them to abandon the Alamo and blow it up so it could not be used by the Mexican army. Although in later years Houston was always careful to praise the defenders of the Alamo for their courage, he never respected their military judgment.

group of 153 men led by Colonel William Barrett Travis took refuge in a 114-year-old Franciscan mission known as the Alamo. With them were about 15 civilians, including the wife of one of the defenders, a black slave, and a few Mexican families who lived there. Santa Anna placed his well-armed troops around the tiny building and launched an intensive assault. The Texans, who were reinforced by 32 men on March 1, withstood the Mexican attack for almost two weeks. On March 6, however, Santa Anna's men were able to force their way into the mission. In the hand-to-hand fighting that followed, 187 of the people inside were killed.

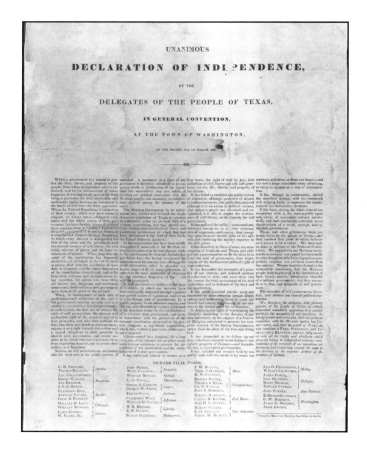

The Texan Declaration of Independence announced, "We . . . the people of Texas, in solemn convention assembled . . . do hereby resolve and declare, that our political connection with the Mexican nation has forever ended, and that the people of Texas, do now constitute a free, sovereign, and independent republic, and are fully invested with all the rights and attributes which properly belong to independent nations."

Houston, meanwhile, was serving as a delegate to Texas's constitutional convention in the town of Washington-on-the-Brazos, where, on March 2, 1836—his 43rd birthday—Texas declared itself an independent republic. On March 11, Houston arrived in the city of Gonzales, where his army of about 400 men awaited him. That same day, he heard the news that the Alamo had been lost. Under Houston's leadership, the army retreated to the banks of the upper Brazos River, where it took a defensive position and waited to see what Santa Anna would do next.

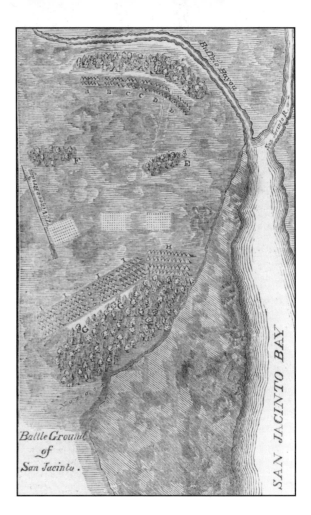

A map of the battleground at San Jacinto shows how greatly the Mexican forces (bottom) outnumbered the Texans (top). Houston gained the advantage of surprise by attacking Santa Anna's camp during the afternoon siesta.

At the Battle of San Jacinto, Texan soldiers also shouted, "Remember Goliad!" On March 27, Mexican soldiers had executed 332 Texan prisoners of war at Goliad.

After a delay of about two weeks, Santa Anna began marching toward the city of Harrisburg, where the provisional government of Texas had established its capital. Immediately, Houston and his much smaller force began marching toward the same point. On April 20, 1836, Houston's force overtook Santa Anna's army at a spot on the banks of the San Jacinto River. The next day, the Texans attacked, shouting "Remember the Alamo!" Taken by surprise, the Mexican army was defeated in less than 20 minutes. But Houston and his officers found that they had lost all control of their men, who went on killing Mexican soldiers for the next several hours. Just 6 of the Texans were slain and 26 wounded, while almost the entire Mexican force of about 1,500 men was killed or captured. One of those captured was Santa Anna, who immediately signed an order instructing all his remaining men to withdraw to Mexico. The settlers in Texas, under the command of General Sam Houston, were victorious.

Houston, meanwhile, was himself a casualty of the battle, shot through the ankle during the attack on the Mexican position. Because of his wound, he was forced to leave his victorious army in the field and go to New Orleans to seek medical attention.

Santa Anna and his top general, Martín Perfecto Cós, surrender to Sam Houston, who is portrayed as a victorious Cherokee chief.

Sam Houston's first official residence as president was hardly more than a cabin—a reminder that Texas was still a wild frontier. The house was located in Houston, a town that had been organized in August 1836 and was named the capital of the Republic of Texas three months later. Although Texas's capital later moved to Austin, the city of Houston continued to thrive; today it is the largest city in Texas and the fourth largest in the U.S.

By the autumn of 1836, Houston was back in Texas. In September, he and Stephen Austin faced off as candidates for the presidency of Texas. Immensely popular because of his role during the Texas Rebellion, Houston easily defeated Austin. Soon after the ballots were counted and Houston became the first president of the Republic of Texas, he took the very unpopular step of freeing Santa Anna and ordering the dictator sent back to Mexico. He also secured the U.S. government's recognition of Texas as an independent republic. Most of his term as president, however, was uneventful.

President Houston's first Official Residence at Houston

Margaret Moffette Lea Houston

After he left office in 1838, Houston's life changed dramatically once again when he married for the third time. He had finally obtained a legal divorce from his first wife in 1837, and Tiana Rogers had died the following year. Houston's third wife, Margaret Lea of Alabama, was an intensely religious woman much younger than Houston. She had a great influence over the way he lived. Almost immediately Houston stopped drinking, at least in public, though he'd been a very heavy drinker from the time he was a young man and was, in all likelihood, an alcoholic. Houston's third marriage was a happy one. The couple had eight children in the years between 1843 and 1860.

Meanwhile, Houston's political career continued. He was elected president of Texas again in 1841, serving until 1844, when he retired from office. In early 1846, after Texas was annexed by the United States, he was elected senator from the new state of Texas. For the next 14 years, Houston served in the Senate, where he was an ardent supporter of the Union in the years leading up to the Civil War. He also continued fighting for the rights of the Native Americans who had been his friends and his family as a young man.

In 1859, after losing his position in the Senate, Houston was elected governor of the state of Texas.

In an annexation ceremony on February 19, 1846, the flag of the Republic of Texas was lowered, to be replaced by the Stars and Stripes of the United States.

As this campaign advertisement shows, Houston ran for governor in 1859 as a pro-Union Democrat. In 1861, however, those same beliefs would make him much less popular in Texas.

By that time, the United States was teetering on the edge of war over the issue of slavery. Houston's goals as governor, he said, were to preserve the Union and to establish a new and fairer Indian policy. Over and over in speeches, he pointed out that war would certainly be the result if any southern states seceded from the Union. He also forecast that if there was a war between the North and South, defeat was inevitable for the southern states.

In 1819, when Texans first sought independence from Mexico, they created a flag very much like that of the United States but with a single, or "lone," star in the upper left corner instead of a field of stars. During the Texas war for independence, a battle flag featured a variation of this "lone star" design. In 1839, three years after the establishment of the Republic of Texas, a flag with a single white star on a vertical blue field was adopted. When Texas joined the Union in 1845, this flag became the official state flag and remains so today.

When Abraham Lincoln was elected president in 1860, the states of the Deep South began to secede from the Union and form the Confederate States of America. In 1861, the people of Texas voted to join the Confederacy, forcing Houston from office because of his pro-Union stance. Called a "hoary-haired traitor" by his enemies, the 68-year-old man retired to his farm not far from Huntsville. There, Houston's life came to an end in 1863.

Though in disfavor with Texans at the time of his death, Sam Houston was once again revered as a hero of the Lone Star State after the passions of the Civil War had cooled. Today, he and Stephen Austin are honored, rightly, as the two men most responsible for the founding and shaping of Texas.

The Lone Star State

In the wake of the Texas Rebellion and the defeat of Mexico's armies, the United States, Great Britain, France, Belgium, and the Netherlands all recognized Texas as an independent republic. The conflict, however, was not over. Soon the Texas settlers were embroiled in a series of wars and skirmishes with Native Americans and also found themselves facing serious financial problems. Seeking help with those difficulties, in July 1845 Texans voted to be annexed by the United States.

At that time, debates were raging across the land about the issue of slavery. Northern lawmakers were unwilling to admit Texas into the Union because it would mean the addition of another state where slavery was legal. Both northerners and southerners, however, were more worried by the British and French diplomats seeking influence over the Republic of Texas. To keep the European powers from gaining a foothold, Congress accepted Texas into the United States despite its slave-state status. In December 1845, it became the 28th state to join the Union.

Just a few months after Texas's annexation, Mexico and the United States were at war as Mexico tried to regain Texas and stop American efforts to acquire California. Within two years (1846-1848), the American army defeated the Mexican forces and the Treaty of Guadalupe Hidalgo was signed. The terms of that treaty required Mexico to cede to the United States two-thirds of its territories and established the Rio Grande River as the border between Mexico and the United States.

After the war with Mexico, Texas claimed that its territory ran from the mouth of the Rio Grande in the Gulf of Mexico to the river's source in southern Colorado. Antislavery advocates opposed this claim because they wanted to keep some of the territory newly acquired from Mexico free of slavery. In 1850, Texas dropped its claim to half of what today is New Mexico and portions of Colorado, Wyoming, Oklahoma, and Kansas. At that time, the state of Texas as we know it today was clearly defined.

Chapter Seven

Eli Thayer
and
Bleeding Kansas

*I*n the 1850s, there was no issue of greater importance in the United States than the future of slavery. In the southern states, where owning slaves was legal, people were terrified that an end to slavery would also mean an end to their cherished way of life. In the northern states, abolitionists were violently opposed to slavery and wanted nothing but to see an end to what was called the "peculiar institution."

In mid-1854, arguments for and against slavery grew even more heated when Stephen Douglas, a U.S. senator from Illinois, proposed what would become the Kansas-Nebraska Act. This act repealed the Missouri Compromise, legislation passed in 1819 that made slavery illegal in the northern part of the territory acquired through the Louisiana Purchase of 1803. Under the terms of the Kansas-Nebraska Act,

Eli Thayer (1819-1899) passionately believed freedom and democracy could be spread throughout the West by settlers who upheld the New England way of life— including abolitionism and technological progress. "The steam engine is a singer, and will sing nothing but freedom," he said in one speech. "Set it sawing pine logs into boards and it will sing at its work day and night, 'Home of the Free. Home of the Free.' Set it to sawing tough gnarled oak and its song will be, 'Never a slave state! Never a slave state!'"

Stephen Douglas (1813-1861) believed that the Union could be preserved peacefully through westward expansion and popular sovereignty (allowing local governments to decide issues like slavery). In 1858, Douglas faced off against Abraham Lincoln for the U.S. Senate seat from Illinois, which Douglas had already held for 10 years. In a series of seven debates, Lincoln opposed the extension of slavery into new territories, while Douglas argued that slavery should be extended if the residents of those territories favored it. Douglas won the election, and in 1860 he ran for president. Once again, his opponent was Abraham Lincoln, but this time Douglas was defeated.

new territories could enter the Union as either proslavery or antislavery, depending upon the will of the people who lived there.

In those troubled times, no one hated slavery more than educator and Massachusetts state legislator Eli Thayer. At every opportunity, he spoke out against the practice of one human legally owning another. When the Kansas-Nebraska legislation was proposed in Congress, Thayer quickly developed a plan to guarantee that the Kansas Territory would enter the Union as a free state. His plan called for the settlement of ardent antislavery groups in Kansas, knowing that these settlers would vote not to allow slavery in the new state. To make his dream of a free Kansas a reality, Thayer and a handful of other abolitionists arranged for some 2,000 settlers to move to what was then the wild frontier. Those settlers eventually founded several communities, including the city of Lawrence, Kansas. Through his role in the settlement of Kansas, Eli Thayer earned a spot in history as one of the shapers of the south-central region of the United States.

Eli Thayer was a native of New England. He was born on June 11, 1819, in the small town of Mendon in eastern Massachusetts, to Cushman and Miranda Thayer. His father, who was a descendant of one of New England's earliest settlers, owned a farm and, later, a country store.

Not much is known of Eli Thayer's youth. Like all farmers' sons, he certainly must have helped his father working in the fields. No doubt, he also spent hours behind the counter in the family's store.

Abolitionists

Men and women who wanted to end slavery in the eighteenth and nineteenth centuries were known as abolitionists. While many of America's earliest settlers—most notably the Quakers who settled Pennsylvania in the late 1600s—believed that slavery was evil, abolitionism did not become a powerful force in America until 1831. In that year, William Lloyd Garrison founded *The Liberator*, an antislavery newspaper in Boston. Two years later, the American Anti-Slavery Society, the most militant abolitionist organization, was organized in Philadelphia under Garrison's leadership.

Many people who were opposed to slavery hoped it would die out over time, but abolitionists wanted an immediate end to slavery. While the movement was united in the goal of ending slavery, it was split over ways to achieve that goal. Some, including Garrison, advocated what they called "moral suasion" to convince slaveholders and others of the evils of slavery. Other abolitionists refused to obey any laws that recognized slavery as a legitimate institution. They helped slaves escape by organizing and operating the Underground Railroad, which concealed runaway slaves and transported them to Canada. Some abolitionists supported direct political or even revolutionary acts of defiance. Among these was John Brown, who led a failed slave revolt in 1859.

Abolitionists eventually helped make the question of whether slavery should be extended to new territories one of the burning issues of the mid-1800s. This, in turn, helped bring about the Civil War and the end of slavery in the United States.

William Lloyd Garrison (1805-1879)

As a teenager, Eli attended Worcester Manual Labor High School, a trade school that later became Worcester Academy. In late 1840, at the age of 21, he enrolled at Brown University in Providence, Rhode Island.

After graduating in 1845, Thayer returned to his old school in Worcester, first as a teacher and later as the academy's principal. During that period, he courted a local young woman, Caroline Capron. They were married on August 6, 1845. During the course of their marriage, the couple had five daughters and two sons.

Eli Thayer was what we would consider an innovator in the field of education. At a time when virtually no women earned college degrees, he believed that young women should have the same opportunity for higher education that men had. To achieve that goal, Thayer founded the Oread Collegiate Institute, a school for young women. The institute was housed in a large building that Thayer had constructed on a hill in Worcester. Complete with round towers at each corner, the "castle," as it was known locally, also served as a residence for Thayer, his wife, and their growing family.

Oread was a remarkable school for its time. It provided women with a four-year college education modeled on the course of study offered by Brown University. Thayer taught both Latin and mathematics to the students at the institute, but he devoted much of his time to politics. Entering public service in about 1848, he held municipal offices in Worcester before being elected to the General

Court—the Massachusetts legislature—where he served in 1853 and 1854. Thayer was a member of the "Free-Soil" party, a political party that opposed allowing slavery in new U.S. territories.

In early 1854, as Congress debated Douglas's Kansas-Nebraska Act, Thayer began what was to be his life's most important work—his plan to make Kansas a free state by colonizing it with abolitionists. He soon convinced a group of like-minded and influential people in the northeastern states to join his cause. Among those he enlisted to help were Amos Lawrence, a wealthy New England textile mill owner, and Horace Greeley, the famous and powerful editor of the *New York Tribune* newspaper.

Abolitionist feeling was running high in Massachusetts in those days, and Thayer's plan soon won the support of the Massachusetts legislature. The legislature approved the creation of the New England Emigrant Aid Company, a group whose guiding principle was that "slavery must not secure another foot of the public domain." Eli Thayer was appointed to the company's board.

It must be noted that while Thayer's primary goal was to fight slavery, he also hoped to make money from his involvement with the Emigrant Aid Company. He wanted to share in the profits made by farming and manufacturing settlements established in the Kansas Territory. In addition, in his job selling stock in the company to investors, Thayer earned ten percent of all the money he collected. By May 1856, the company had received over $100,000.

Horace Greeley (1811-1872) was a crusading journalist and an ardent abolitionist who urged the settlement of what was then the western frontier and coined the famous phrase, "Go West, young man."

To achieve his goals, Thayer traveled extensively throughout New England, promoting the company and recruiting supporters. At the same time, he and the other members of the company board hired Charles Robinson, a one-time settler in California, to explore the Kansas Territory and choose a site for the Emigrant Aid Company's first settlement. In early July 1854, Robinson found the spot he was looking for in a green valley about 35 miles west of the present-day site of Kansas City, Kansas. He sent word back to New England that settlers could now be sent to found their antislavery township.

Charles Robinson (1818-1894) eventually became the first governor of the state of Kansas.

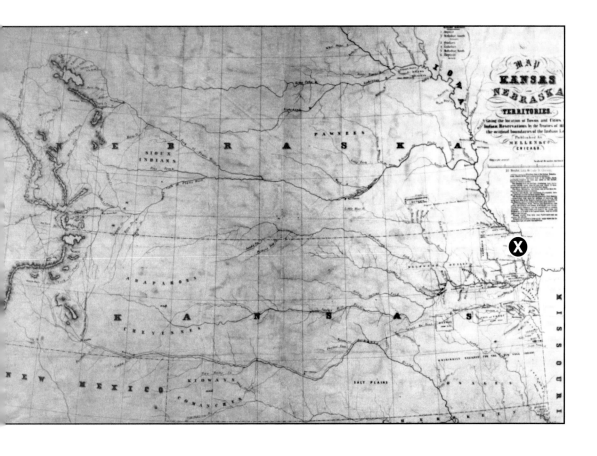

An 1855 map of the Kansas and Nebraska Territories, with the site of Robinson's free-soil settlement marked by an "X"

The Emigrant Aid Company wasted no time. On July 17, almost within hours of receiving word from Robinson, 29 men left Boston and headed west by rail and riverboat to St. Louis, Missouri, the jumping-off point for almost all west-bound travelers in those days. There, they loaded wagons with supplies, which included tents, bedding, and a printing press to be used in spreading the abolitionist message. Guided by an agent of the Emigrant Aid Company, they made their way west to the site chosen by Robinson.

Kansas before Thayer

Francisco Vásquez de Coronado became the first European to set foot in Kansas when he explored the area in 1541. At that time, what would become Kansas was home to three major Native American tribes, the Kansa (who gave their name to the state), the Osage, and the Pawnee. The introduction of domesticated horses to the region by Spanish explorers helped these Plains Indians to hunt buffalo more efficiently, and they developed a complex culture that reached its peak in the late 1700s.

For many years, the Native Americans of Kansas were otherwise undisturbed by Europeans. Far from the earliest settlements of France, Spain, and England, the region was not very attractive because it was so difficult to reach. Indeed, serious attempts at exploring the region did not start until the early 1800s, following the purchase of the Louisiana territory by the United States in 1803.

After this time, expeditions were sent out to explore the West, and many passed through what we now know as Kansas. Zebulon Pike, an Army lieutenant who led an exploratory expedition to New Mexico and who discovered Pike's Peak in Colorado, visited Kansas in 1806. Major Stephen Long also came through Kansas while exploring the region between the Missouri River and the Rocky Mountains in 1819 and 1820.

Long, for some reason, used the term "Great American Desert" to describe what we know as the Great Plains of America, one of the richest farming regions in the world. Thanks to Long's erroneous description of the region, Kansas was for many years considered an unlikely place for settlement. Instead, the U.S. government used the land to establish reservations for Indians moved from their own lands in the East.

For many years, Kansas was merely a region to be crossed by westward-bound traders and pioneers on the Santa Fe Trail. Over time, however, forts began to be built in the area: Fort Leavenworth in 1827, Fort Scott in 1842, and Fort Riley in 1853. Eventually, travelers passing through Kansas realized that the region was ideal for settlement. Soon, pressure built to open the area to land-hungry immigrants. In the early 1850s, Indians living in Kansas were moved to what would become the state of Oklahoma. In 1854, the government opened Kansas to settlement under the terms of the Kansas-Nebraska Act.

Soon, these New Englanders and others who followed had established a thriving tent city in the wilderness. At first, this settlement was called Wakarusa, after a stream that ran nearby. Opponents of abolitionism called it Yankee Town. Robinson officially named the town Lawrence, after Amos Lawrence, the Emigrant Aid Company's major financial backer. During the summer of 1854, the company settled five more groups of eastern immigrants in Kansas—about 600 people in all.

Of course, supporters of slavery were not about to sit on the sidelines and watch as groups of abolitionists from New England settled the Kansas Territory. Proslavery settlers from Missouri were also moving into the region in the hope of making Kansas a slave state. The question of whether slavery

Among the original inhabitants of Kansas were the Kansa Indians.

When the first abolitionists arrived in Kansas, they received a note from proslavery Missourians warning them to leave within an hour or suffer the consequences. As Robinson scribbled a defiant answer, one of the abolitionist settlers asked him, "Will you fire over their heads or to kill if they decide to come?" "I'd be ashamed to fire at a man and not hit him," Robinson replied.

Lawrence in 1858, the year it was incorporated

❖

"To those having qualms of conscience as to violating laws, state or national, the time has come when such impositions must be disregarded. Your lives and property are in danger, and I advise you one and all to enter every election district in Kansas . . . and vote at the point of a Bowie knife or pistol."
—John Stringfellow, editor of a proslavery newspaper, to a crowd in St. Joseph, Missouri

❖

would be allowed in Kansas was to be determined by what was known as "popular sovereignty"—in other words, Kansans would decide the issue by vote. During voting to elect the territorial legislature in 1855, however, several thousand proslavery voters crossed the border from Missouri and proceeded to stuff ballot boxes, often threatening election officials at gunpoint. The situation was so bad during this rigged election that although there were only 2,905 legitimate voters in the territory, some 6,028 ballots were cast. "We had at least seven thousand men in the Territory on the day of the election," bragged proslavery Senator David Atchison of Missouri after the voting. "The pro-slavery ticket prevailed everywhere. . . . Now let the Southern men come on with their slaves. Ten thousand families can take possession of and hold every acre . . . in the Territory of Kansas, and this secures the prairie. . . . If we win, we carry slavery to the Pacific Ocean."

Naturally enough, the free-soilers considered the election of 1855 fraudulent and went so far as to establish their own government. They knew that armed conflict between themselves and the proslavery settlers was inevitable. Quickly, Robinson wrote to Eli Thayer asking him to supply the Lawrence settlers with a new kind of rifle, the Sharp's breechloader, so that they could defend themselves against the proslavery forces.

Proslavery Missourians willing to travel to Kansas to cast ballots in the 1855 election were promised "free ferry [transportation], a dollar a day, and liquor."

THE DAY OF
OUR ENSLAVEMENT!!

To-day, Sept. 15, 1855, is the day on which the ini-
quitous enactment of an illegitimate, illegal and fraudulent Legislature have declared commences the prostration of the Right of Speech and the curtailment of the **LIBERTY OF THE PRESS!!** To-day commences an Era in Kansas which, unless the sturdy voice of the People, backed, if necessary, by "strong arms and the sure eye," shall teach the ty-rants who attempt to enthrall us the lesson which our Fathers taught to kingly tyrants of old, shall prostrate us in the dust, and make us the slaves of an Oligarchy

Worse than the veriest Despotism on Earth!

To-day commences the operation of a law which declares: "Sec. 12. If any free person, by speaking or by writing, as-sert or maintain that persons have not the right to hold slaves in this Territory, or shall introduce into this Territory, print, publish, write, circulate or cause to be introduced into this Territory, written, printed, published or circulated in this Territory, any book, paper, magazine, pamphlet or circular, containing any denial of the right of persons to hold slaves in this Territory, such person shall be deemed guilty of Felony, and punished by imprisonment at hard labor for a term of not less than two years."

Now we DO ASSERT and we declare, despite all the
bolts and bars of the iniquitous Legislature of Kansas, that

"PERSONS HAVE NOT THE
RIGHT TO HOLD SLAVES IN THIS
TERRITORY."

And we will emblazon it upon our banner in letters so large and in language so plain that the infatuated invaders who elected the Kansas Legislature, as well as

THAT CORRUPT AND IGNORANT LEGISLATURE

Itself, may understand it — so that, if they cannot read,
they may **SPELL IT OUT**, and meditate and deliberate upon it; and we hold that the man who fails to utter this self-evident truth, on account of the insolent enactment alluded to, is a poltroon and a slave worse than the black slaves of our persecutors and oppressors.

The Constitution of the United States, the great Magna Charta of American Liberties,

Guarantees to every Citizen the Liberty of Speech and
the Freedom of the Press!

And this is the first time in the history of America that a body claiming Legislative powers has dared to attempt to wrest them from the people. And it is not only the right, but the bounden duty of every Freeman to spurn with contempt and trample under foot an enactment which thus basely violates the rights of Freemen. For our part we **DO** and **SHALL CONTINUE** to utter this truth so long as we have the power of utterance, and nothing but the brute force of an over-bearing tyranny can prevent us.

Will any citizen — any free American — brook the insult of

AN INSOLENT GAG LAW!!

the work of a Legislature elected by bullying ruffians who invaded Kansas with arms, and whose drunken revelry, and insults to our peaceable, unoffending, and comparatively unarmed citizens, were a disgrace to manhood, and a burlesque upon popular Republican Government! If they do, they are slaves already, and with them Freedom is but a mockery.

This page from the Lawrence-based Kansas Tribune *protests the "bogus" proslavery legislature elected in 1855 "by bullying ruffians who invaded Kansas with arms, and whose drunken revelry and insults to our peaceable, unoffending, and comparatively unarmed citizens, were a disgrace to manhood."*

By late 1855, the free-state and proslavery forces were engaged in periodic fighting. While there were no great battles in what is often called the Kansas War, there was unending violence for an entire decade. Early in the conflict, supporters of slavery—led by, among others, former senator Atchison—attacked and destroyed Lawrence, the city founded by settlers that Eli Thayer had sent to Kansas. Following the raid on Lawrence, a fanatic abolitionist named John Brown wreaked vengeance when he and several followers hacked five proslavery settlers to death with cutlasses.

Kansas held one election after another to try to decide whether to allow slavery, and each was marked by illegal voting. The elections became so frequent, people joked that Kansan babies should be born with ballot boxes attached to them.

Armed with a cannon, free-state settlers prepare to fight for their beliefs.

This political cartoon, published during the 1856 presidential campaign, criticizes the Democratic U.S. government for igniting the violence in Kansas. Democrats such as President Franklin Pierce, presidential candidate James Buchanan, and Stephen Douglas are shown as bloodthirsty "border ruffians" terrorizing innocent settlers and a woman symbolizing "Liberty."

The United States divided over the questions of slavery and popular sovereignty in the territory that had become known as "Bleeding Kansas." Whether Kansas entered the Union as a free state or a slave state seemed to decide the fate of the entire nation. Abolitionists (mainly in the North) and proslavery leaders in the South took firm positions on the issue and were unwilling to bend. The fighting that tore Kansas apart grew into a widespread debate, inflaming the passions that would ignite the Civil War just six years later.

Eli Thayer never did visit Kansas, though 1,240 settlers were sent there by the organization he founded. In addition to the town of Lawrence, these Emigrant Aid Company pioneers founded or helped to found several other Kansas communities, including Osawatomie, Manhattan, Leavenworth, and Topeka.

Although the abolitionists sent west were harassed or even killed by proslavery mobs, Thayer continued to believe that emigration sponsored by the New England Emigrant Aid Company could cure a variety of social problems. It was his belief, for example, that company-backed settlers sent to

Some of the many settlers who began a new life in Kansas

Utah, where Mormons had already founded Salt Lake City, would soon force an end to polygamy (the Mormon practice of multiple marriages). Thayer even believed that abolitionist settlements could bring about the end of slavery in so-called "border states" such as Virginia.

During the period when support for abolitionism ran highest, Thayer, the former schoolmaster, was elected to the U.S. Congress as a representative from Massachusetts, running on the ticket of the newly formed Republican Party. He served two terms, from 1857 to 1861. According to witnesses, he was a witty and engaging speaker. His single-minded focus on using settlers to bring about change, however, made him unpopular with the Republican Party, which was in favor of ending slavery through federal legislation. In 1860, forced to run as an independent, Thayer lost his seat.

During his years in Congress, Thayer came into contact with John Brown, the radical abolitionist who had been a ringleader in the killing of five proslavery settlers in Kansas. Brown visited Thayer in Worcester and asked for weapons that he said would be used to help defend free-state settlers in Kansas. Thayer, not surprisingly, gave Brown all the weapons he had at his disposal. Eventually, these same weapons were used in Brown's ill-conceived attack on the U.S. Army armory at Harpers Ferry, Virginia, on October 16, 1859. For the rest of his life, Thayer was openly bitter about the fact that Brown had tricked him into providing arms for an act he considered treasonous.

The Republican Party was founded in 1854 by people who opposed the extension of slavery into the territories of Kansas and Nebraska. The party was composed mainly of Whigs (members of a political party formed in the 1830s to fight the policies of President Andrew Jackson) and some former Democrats. In pre-Civil-War America, Republicans were advocates of a strong central government. They were also opposed to immigrants coming to the United States from other nations. The other major political party then—as now—was the Democratic Party. In the 1850s, it was made up largely of proslavery advocates who believed strongly in states' rights and were fearful of consolidating the power of the federal government.

During the Civil War, Thayer occupied a series of minor government posts. Following the war, he spent several years as a land agent in New York, working for railroads that were establishing lines to serve the rapidly expanding western frontier. He ran for Congress in 1874 and 1878, but was defeated both times.

Hoping that their raid would spark a widespread slave rebellion, John Brown and 18 other radical abolitionists held Harpers Ferry (with a few local citizens as hostages) for two days before being captured. Brown was tried and hanged two months later.

Eli Thayer lived for 20 more years, dying on April 15, 1899. During the last years of his life, he was a bitter and unhappy man. He always felt that his contribution to the early settlement of Kansas had been overlooked and that his role in establishing Kansas as a free state had never been properly recognized. Indeed, Thayer has been largely forgotten, despite the fact that it was his founding of the Emigrant Aid Company to send settlers west that transformed Kansas from a vast, empty prairie into a thriving state.

Kansas after the Civil War

Entering the Union as a free state on January 29, 1861, Kansas continued to be troubled by conflicts between proslavery settlers and abolitionists throughout the years of the Civil War. Consequently, settlement was slow in the region.

Soon after the end of the Civil War, however, the rate of settlement increased dramatically. Several years of good rainfall made the region's rich soil very attractive to settlers from the East. By the 1870s, a major land boom was underway as railroad construction moved westward. Kansas towns such as Abilene and Dodge City grew into major shipping points for cattle, which were driven overland from Texas and sent by railroad to cities in the East. Many of the 347,000 settlers who came to Kansas in those years were immigrants from Germany, Sweden, and Russia. Russian immigrants brought a variety of winter wheat that thrived in Kansas, boosting the state's agricultural production. By 1880, Kansas had nearly 850,000 residents.

Periods of prosperous farming in Kansas were interrupted by natural disasters, including droughts, dust storms, grasshopper invasions, and floods. In the 1930s, a long period of drought coupled with strong winds howling across thousands of acres of unprotected soil turned the Great Plains, including Kansas, into what was known as the "Dust Bowl." Since that time, however, improved agricultural techniques have made Kansas once again one of the world's leading farming areas.

The Settlement of Nebraska

One of the major reasons for the 1854 Kansas-Nebraska Act was to create a route for a proposed transcontinental railroad. Northerners, who wanted the railroad to pass through a north-central part of the country rather than through the South, hurried to organize the Great Plains lands and settle the question of slavery there. The act's sponsor, Stephen Douglas, divided the area into two territories, figuring that the southern one (Kansas) would become a slave state while the northern one (Nebraska) became a free state—and an ideal site for building the railroad.

Originally inhabited by Pawnee and Omaha Indians, Nebraska had seen little European settlement; its few communities were based on trade. In the early nineteenth century, fur traders built trading posts such as Bellvue (the first permanent settlement in the area), while steamboats on the Missouri River soon brought business to river ports like Omaha. The U.S. Army established Fort Atkinson, its westernmost outpost, in Nebraska in 1819 to protect trade there. Several decades later, pioneers on the Oregon Trail, the California Trail, and the Mormon Trail began to pass through Nebraska, and outposts such as Kearney City and Grand Island sprang up along those routes to sell supplies to travelers.

Settlement of Nebraska increased after the Kansas-Nebraska Act, and in 1863 the territory—which originally had stretched north to the Canadian border—was reduced to its present size. In 1867, Nebraska became a state (its capital at the time was Omaha, but it later moved to Lincoln), and the Union Pacific Railroad was built across it. These two events launched an enormous rush for land, doubling Nebraska's population.

The region's lands were ideal for both farming and ranching, but a series of natural disasters—including cold winters, insects, prairies fires, and droughts—often caused economic depression. The state continued to draw settlers, however, including a huge influx of Irish, Swedish, and German immigrants that brought the population up to one million by 1890.

Indian Territory and the State of Oklahoma

The earliest known residents of the land we know today as Oklahoma were nomadic hunters who lived in the region some 15,000 years ago. Among the descendants of these early people were Native Americans of the mound-builder civilization. A large mound-builder settlement called Spiro was located in eastern Oklahoma near the border of present-day Arkansas.

After the decline of Spiro around A.D. 1300, Native Americans from the western plains began to move into Oklahoma. Among these newcomers were nomadic tribes such as the Osage, Kiowa Apache, and Comanche. The Wichita, who inhabited the western part of the region, were farmers who lived in small villages located along rivers.

The first European to visit the area was the Spanish explorer Francisco Vásquez de Coronado, who crossed the western part of the region in 1541. After Coronado's expedition, other Spanish explorers visited western and southern Oklahoma, while French adventurers explored the eastern part of the region. None of these early visitors stayed long, however. It was not until 1796 that the first European settlement was established when Jean Pierre Chouteau, the half brother of Auguste Chouteau, established a trading post at what is now Salina, Oklahoma.

In 1803, the Oklahoma region became part of the United States when the U.S. government purchased all the land between the Mississippi River and the Rocky Mountains from France. In the period that followed the Louisiana Purchase, Oklahoma came to play a central role in the history of Native Americans in the United States.

As the nation grew in size and power during the early 1800s, pressure began building on the U.S. government to do something about the Native American people living east of the Mississippi River. These tribes occupied valuable land that settlers wanted. Many white Americans believed that the Indians should be removed from these lands to areas in the West. In the 1820s, government officials proposed that the eastern tribes be moved to the Oklahoma region, which would become a permanent reserve for them. Eventually this area, along with large parts of present-day Kansas and Nebraska, would be designated as the Indian Territory.

In 1830, the relocation of eastern Indians became the law of the land when, at the urging of President Andrew Jackson, the U.S. Congress passed the Indian Removal Act. This act provided for the relocation of thousands of Indians from western North and South Carolina, eastern

Tennessee, Georgia, Florida, Alabama, and Mississippi. It made no difference to the government or to settlers that these lands were home to the so-called Five Civilized Tribes, the Choctaw, Chickasaw, Creek, Seminole, and Cherokee. Many of these Native Americans had tried to adapt to European-American ways, living very much as whites did. Nevertheless, they had to be moved to make way for white settlers.

To implement the removal plan, the federal government began negotiating with the tribes to exchange their eastern lands for reservations in the Indian Territory. As a result of these negotiations, thousands of Indian people were persuaded, tricked, or simply forced to give up their lands to make room for whites.

Of course, settling Indians from the East in the Indian Territory required cooperation from Native Americans already living there. To gain this cooperation, the U.S. signed a series of treaties with the Comanche, Wichita, Kiowa Apache, and other tribes in the Oklahoma region. These treaties required the Oklahoma Indians to live on reservations within the Indian Territory and not to wage war on the eastern tribes or on whites traveling through the area. Despite the treaties, conflict was common in the region.

In 1854, the Indian Territory was greatly reduced in size when the northern section became the Kansas and Nebraska

territories and the Native Americans living there were forced into the southern section, present-day Oklahoma. In the following years, more and more Indian tribes, including nomadic hunters of the

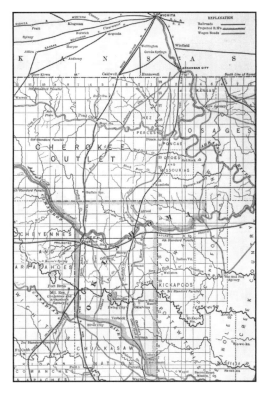

This 1889 map of the area that became Oklahoma shows the complex division of land between tribes of Native Americans from all over the United States, including the Osage, Cherokee, Cheyenne, Seminole, and Comanche.

Great Plains such as the Cheyenne, were forced to move from their homes to live on specified lands in the Indian Territory. By the 1880s, about 31 tribes had reservations in the region.

At that time, pressure was building to open the Indian Territory to settlers. The land had earlier been considered undesirable, but now whites were taking a second look at it. Many white people had already come to the Oklahoma region to work on farms and ranches leased from the Indian tribes. But they wanted to own the land, and this was illegal in Indian Territory.

In 1887, the U.S. Congress passed an act that would pave the way for settlement of the Indian Territory. The General Allotment Act (called the Dawes Act after its sponsor in Congress) called for reservation lands to be divided into small parcels that would be assigned, or allotted, to individual Indians. The Dawes Act was intended to help "Americanize" Indians by making them independent landowners like other Americans. One of its results, however, was the opening up of tribal lands for settlement. After each head of an Indian household was allotted 160 acres, as the Dawes Act required, large amounts of "surplus" reservation land were left—as much as 90 percent on some reservations. This land could be purchased by the federal government and offered to settlers.

In early 1889, before the allotment system was put into effect, the U.S. government decided to allow some settlers into the "unassigned lands" of the Indian Territory, a central area not occupied by any tribe. This land was made available under the 1862 Homestead Act, which gave 160-acre homesteads to would-be settlers for $1.25 an acre, provided the land was worked for a specified period of time.

So many settlers wanted land in Indian Territory that it was decided the only fair way to allocate homesteads was to hold a "horse race," or "run," from the border of the region to be settled. Participants in the race could stake their claims on a first-come, first-served basis. These settlers became known as "boomers" because of their role in the Oklahoma land boom. Some settlers, hungry for land, cheated by moving into areas being opened for settlement before the appointed date and time. They were called "sooners."

The first of the runs took place on April 22, 1889. According to witnesses, 50,000 hopeful settlers took part in the frantic race to claim the unassigned lands. A year later, the area where whites had settled was declared the Oklahoma Territory. During the next few years, the Oklahoma Territory gradually expanded and the Indian Territory shrank as tribal lands were distributed in allotments and the surplus offered to settlers. In 1893, the largest of

"Boomers" entering Oklahoma Territory to claim land for homesteads

the land rushes occurred when the so-called Cherokee Outlet, six million acres located in the northwestern region, was opened for settlement. About 100,000 boomers rushed in to stake claims.

During the late 1800s and early 1900s, the region's white population grew rapidly, and settlers began to press for statehood.

Finally, in 1907, the few remaining sections of the Indian Territory were merged with the Oklahoma Territory to form the state of Oklahoma. On November 16, 1907, Oklahoma became the 46th state of the Union. Ironically, the name of the new state came from a phrase in the Choctaw language meaning "home of the red people."

A South-Central Timeline

1519: Spanish explorer Alonso Álvarez de Piñeda becomes the first known European to visit Texas and to see the Mississippi River.

1528-1536: Álvar Nuñez Cabeza de Vaca leads a group of explorers through the Southwest, including Texas.

1541: Hernando de Soto explores the Southeast, including Arkansas and Tennessee; Francisco Vásquez de Coronado visits Texas, Kansas, and Oklahoma on a journey through the Southwest.

1649 or 1650: Henry de Tonty is born, possibly in Gaeta, Italy.

1673: French explorers Louis Joliet and Jacques Marquette visit Arkansas and Missouri.

September 15, 1678: Tonty arrives in Quebec with Robert de La Salle to begin exploring North America.

April 7, 1682: Tonty and La Salle arrive at the mouth of the Mississippi River.

1682: The first European settlement in Texas is founded by the Spanish at Ysleta.

1685: Shipwrecked in Texas, La Salle establishes a French settlement at Fort St. Louis.

1686: Tonty establishes Arkansas Post.

1689: A conflict begins between Britain and France that will become the French and Indian War.

1704: Tonty dies of yellow fever in Mobile, Alabama.

1720: John Law promotes settlement at Arkansas Post.

November 2, 1734: Daniel Boone is born in Pennsylvania.

1735: The first European settlement in Missouri is founded at Ste. Genevieve.

September 23, 1745: John Sevier is born in the Shenandoah Valley of Virginia.

September 1749: Auguste Chouteau is born in New Orleans.

1750: Dr. Thomas Walker discovers and names the Cumberland Gap.

July 9, 1755: Boone fights in the Battle of Fort Duquesne in the French and Indian War.

1756: The British establish Fort Loudoun in Tennessee, their first settlement west of the Smoky Mountains.

1762: In the Treaty of Fontainbleu, France cedes all its possessions west of the Mississippi River to Spain in exchange for help in the French and Indian War.

February 10, 1763: The Treaty of Paris ends the French and Indian War, giving England control of all lands east of the Mississippi River.

February 14, 1764: Chouteau begins construction of St. Louis in Missouri.

1768: Iroquois Indians cede the Kentucky lands to the British.

May 1, 1769: Boone departs on his first visit to Kentucky.

Early 1770s: **Chouteau** becomes a full partner in his stepfather's prosperous Missouri fur-trading business.

1772: The Watauga Association is formed to govern Tennessee.

December 25, 1773: **Sevier** settles his family in the Watauga region of Tennessee.

1774: Lord Dunmore's War is fought between white settlers and the Native Americans of Kentucky and Tennessee.

March 1775: **Boone** builds a road into Kentucky and establishes the settlement of Boonesborough.

1775-1783: The American colonies fight for independence from England in the Revolutionary War.

July 1776: **Sevier** defends Fort Watauga.

1776: The Watauga region of Tennessee becomes part of North Carolina.

February 9, 1778: **Boone** and his men are captured by the Shawnee; about four months later, he escapes to warn the settlers that the Shawnee and the British are planning to attack Boonesborough.

1779: **Boone** leads more settlers into Kentucky, founding Boone's Station.

October 6, 1780: **Sevier** commands American troops in the Battle of King's Mountain against the British.

1782: **Boone** fights in the Battle of Blue Licks.

1784: North Carolina cedes Tennessee to the Continental Congress.

1785: Three Tennessee counties, at the time part of North Carolina, form the independent state of Franklin.

1790: The state of Franklin is joined with the rest of Tennessee, becoming "The Territory of the United States South of the River Ohio."

June 1, 1792: Kentucky becomes the 15th state in the Union.

March 2, 1793: **Samuel Houston** is born in Virginia.

November 3, 1793: **Stephen Austin** is born in Virginia.

June 1, 1796: Tennessee becomes the 16th state in the Union.

1796: Jean Pierre Chouteau builds the first European settlement in Oklahoma.

1797: **Sevier** becomes the first governor of Tennessee.

1800: Spain cedes the Louisiana territory west of the Mississippi River back to France.

April 30, 1803: The United States buys the Louisiana territory from France.

1806: American explorer Zebulon Pike visits Kansas and Nebraska.

1808: The village of St. Louis is incorporated; **Chouteau** is elected chairman of its board of trustees.

1812: The Missouri Territory is formed.

1812-1814: The United States fights Britain in the War of 1812.

March 28, 1814: **Houston** fights Creek Indians allied with the British in the Battle of Horseshoe Bend.

1815: **Sevier** dies in Alabama.

June 11, 1819: **Eli Thayer** is born in Massachusetts.

1819: The Arkansas Territory is created, with Arkansas Post as its capital.

1819: The U.S. Army establishes Fort Atkinson, its westernmost outpost at the time, in Nebraska.

1819-1820: American explorer Stephen Long visits Kansas and Nebraska, labeling the area the "Great American Desert."

September 26, 1820: Boone dies in Missouri.

August 10, 1821: Missouri becomes the 24th state in the Union under the terms of the Missouri Compromise, which allows slavery in the southern half of the U.S.

August 24, 1821: Mexico wins independence from Spain and takes control of Spanish territories in North America.

1823: The Mexican government grants **Austin** the land for an American colony in Texas.

1825: The Mexican government passes a law encouraging American immigration to Texas and offering generous land grants to colonists.

1827: Houston is elected governor of Tennessee.

1827: Cherokee Indians form the Cherokee Nation.

February 24, 1829: Chouteau dies in St. Louis, the city he founded.

April 6, 1830: The Mexican government passes a law forbidding further American immigration to Texas and increasing military garrisons there.

1830: President Andrew Jackson signs the Indian Removal Act, forcing eastern Native Americans to give up their land and move west to the Indian Territory, which includes present-day Oklahoma and parts of Kansas and Nebraska.

1831: William Lloyd Garrison founds *The Liberator*, launching the abolitionist movement.

1832: Houston arrives in Texas and buys land in **Austin**'s colony.

April 1, 1833: Antonio López de Santa Anna becomes president of Mexico. On the same day, Texans—including **Austin** and **Houston**—meet at San Felipe de Austin and decide to seek recognition as a separate Mexican state.

June 1, 1833: Austin departs for Mexico City to present the Texan grievances to the government. During his return journey, he is arrested by the Mexicans and imprisoned for 18 months.

October 2, 1835: The Battle of Gonzales begins the Texan war for independence.

November 1835: Austin travels to Washington, D.C., to seek American aid for Texas, and **Houston** becomes commander of the Texan army.

March 2, 1836: Texas declares independence from Mexico.

March 6, 1836: The Mexican army defeats the Texan defenders of the Alamo.

April 20, 1836: Houston leads Texan troops to victory in the Battle of San Jacinto, ending the war in Texas.

June 15, 1836: Arkansas becomes the 25th state in the Union.

September 5, 1836: Houston defeats **Austin** in the election of the first president of the Republic of Texas.

December 27, 1836: Austin dies in Texas.

1838: The Cherokee are forcibly removed from their lands in Georgia to the Indian Territory in present-day Oklahoma on a march known as the Trail of Tears.

July 4, 1845: Texas is annexed by the United States.

December 29, 1845: Texas becomes the 28th state in the Union.

May 13, 1846: The United States declares war on Mexico over territory in Texas and the Southwest.

February 2, 1848: The Treaty of Guadalupe Hidalgo ends the Mexican War, giving the United States vast amounts of land in Texas and the Southwest.

1853: Thayer is elected to the Massachusetts legislature, where he is a member of the abolitionist Free-Soil Party.

May 30, 1854: The Kansas-Nebraska Act creates the territories of Kansas and Nebraska out of parts of the Indian Territory, leaving the issue of slavery up to the settlers.

July 17, 1854: The first "free-soil" settlers sponsored by **Thayer**'s New England Emigrant Aid Company depart for Kansas.

1855: Illegal voting in the election of Kansas's territorial legislature leads to a proslavery victory, Kansas abolitionists form their own government, and the Kansas War begins.

October 16, 1859: John Brown leads a failed raid on the federal arsenal at Harpers Ferry, Virginia, in the hope of inspiring a slave rebellion.

1859: Houston is elected governor of Texas.

January 29, 1861: Kansas becomes the 34th state in the Union.

1861: Texas secedes from the Union; Governor **Houston** refuses to swear allegiance to the Confederacy and is removed from office.

1861-1865: The Civil War is fought.

May 20, 1862: The Homestead Act is passed, giving settlers the right to claim up to 160 acres of public land after residing on it for a certain amount of time.

July 26, 1863: Houston dies in Texas.

March 1, 1867: Nebraska becomes the 37th state in the Union.

1887: The General Allotment Act, or Dawes Act, is passed with the intention of reorganizing lands in the Indian Territory to make room for white settlement.

April 22, 1889: The first "run" or "horse race" is held in the Indian Territory, allowing white settlers to claim unoccupied lands in its western half. A few months later, this area becomes the Oklahoma Territory.

April 15, 1899: Thayer dies.

November 16, 1907: The remaining Indian Territory is merged with the Oklahoma Territory to form Oklahoma, the 46th state in the Union.

Source Notes

Quoted passages are noted by page and order of citation.

Chapter One

p. 15 (margin): Edmund R. Murphy, *Henry de Tonty: Fur Trader of the Mississippi* (Baltimore: Johns Hopkins Press, 1941), 9.

p. 17 (first margin): T. J. Stiles, ed., *In Their Own Words: The Colonizers* (New York: Perigee, 1998), 279-280.

p. 17 (second margin): Murphy, *Henry de Tonty*, 13.

p. 17: Stiles, *In Their Own Words*, 280.

p. 18 (caption): Ted Morgan, *Wilderness at Dawn: The Settling of the North American Continent* (New York: Simon & Schuster, 1993), 200.

p. 21 (margin): Morgan, *Wilderness at Dawn*, 201.

p. 21: Stiles, *In Their Own Words*, 282.

p. 22 (margin): Stiles, *In Their Own Words*, 282.

p. 23 (margin): Stiles, *In Their Own Words*, 285.

pp. 25-26: Murphy, *Henry de Tonty*, 36.

Chapter Two

p. 36 (margin): Stanley Vestal, *The Missouri* (New York: Farrar and Rinehart, 1945), 11.

p. 36: William E. Foley and C. David Rice, *The First Chouteaus: River Barons of Early St. Louis* (Urbana: Univ. of Illinois, 1983), 5.

p. 45: Foley and Rice, *The First Chouteaus*, 24.

Chapter Three

p. 52: John Mack Faragher, *Daniel Boone: The Life and Legend of an American Pioneer* (New York: Holt, 1992), 15.

p. 54 (margin): Faragher, *Daniel Boone*, 66.

p. 55 (margin): Faragher, *Daniel Boone*, 79.

p. 59 (all): Faragher, *Daniel Boone*, 114.

p. 61 (margin): Faragher, *Daniel Boone*, 143.

p. 62 (caption): Faragher, *Daniel Boone*, 137.

p. 63 (margin): Faragher, *Daniel Boone*, 205.

p. 64 (margin): John Bakeless, *Daniel Boone* (Harrisburg, Pa.: Stackpole, 1939), 245-246.

p. 67 (caption): Faragher, *Daniel Boone*, 7.

p. 67 (margin): Faragher, *Daniel Boone*, 225.

p. 70 (margin): Faragher, *Daniel Boone*, 39.

p. 71: Faragher, *Daniel Boone*, 318-319.

Chapter Four

p. 84 (margin): Morgan, *Wilderness at Dawn*, 454.

p. 87 (margin): Francis Marion Turner, *Life of General John Sevier* (Johnson City, Tenn.: Overmountain Press, 1997), 101.

p. 90: Turner, *Life of General John Sevier*, 126.

Chapter Five

p. 93 (caption): Eugene C. Barker, *The Life of Stephen F. Austin* (Nashville: Cokesbury, 1925), 524, 520.

p. 93: Barker, *The Life of Stephen F. Austin*, 31.

p. 94: Barker, *The Life of Stephen F. Austin*, 20.

p. 95 (caption): Barker, *The Life of Stephen F. Austin*, 28.

p. 97 (first margin): John E. and Jane Weems, *Dream of Empire: A Human History of the Republic of Texas, 1836-1846* (New York: Simon & Schuster, 1971), 25.

p. 97 (second margin): Barker, *The Life of Stephen F. Austin*, 49.

p. 97: Barker, *The Life of Stephen F. Austin*, 61.

p. 100 (caption): Barker, *The Life of Stephen F. Austin*, 100.

p. 101 (margin): Barker, *The Life of Stephen F. Austin*, 117.

p. 101: Barker, *The Life of Stephen F. Austin*, 116.

p. 103 (margin): Barker, *The Life of Stephen F. Austin*, 254.

p. 104: Barker, *The Life of Stephen F. Austin*, 261.

p. 106 (margin): Barker, *The Life of Stephen F. Austin*, 437.

p. 107 (caption): Barker, *The Life of Stephen F. Austin*, 47.

p. 107: W. J. Ghent, *The Early Far West: A Narrative Outline, 1540-1850* (New York: Longmans, Green, 1931), 270.

p. 111 (all): Barker, *The Life of Stephen F. Austin*, 520.

Chapter Six

p. 113: Marshall De Bruhl, *Sword of San Jacinto: A Life of Sam Houston* (New York: Random House, 1993), 402.

p. 120 (caption): De Bruhl, *Sword of San Jacinto*, 43.

p. 124 (margin): De Bruhl, *Sword of San Jacinto*, 169.

p. 134: Dumas Malone, ed., *Dictionary of American Biography*, Vol. 5 (New York: Scribner's, 1961), 267.

Chapter Seven

p. 137 (caption): Jay Monaghan, *Civil War on the Western Border* (Boston: Little, Brown, 1955), 6.

p. 141: Ted Morgan, A *Shovel of Stars: The Making of the American West, 1800 to the Present* (New York: Simon & Schuster, 1995), 199.

p. 142 (margin): Monaghan, *Civil War on the Western Border*, 12.

p. 145 (margin): Monaghan, *Civil War on the Western Border*, 11.

p. 146 (margin): Alice Nichols, *Bleeding Kansas* (New York: Oxford University Press, 1954), 27.

pp. 146-147: Samuel Eliot Morison, Henry Steele Commager, and William E. Luechtenburg, *The Growth of the American Republic*, Vol. 1 (New York: Oxford University Press, 1980), 589-590.

p. 147 (caption): Nichols, *Bleeding Kansas*, 26.

Bibliography

Bakeless, John. *America as Seen by Its First Explorers*. New York: Dover Publications, 1961.

———. *Daniel Boone*. Harrisburg, Pa.: Stackpole, 1939.

Barker, Eugene C. *The Life of Stephen F. Austin*. Nashville: Cokesbury, 1925.

Billington, Ray Allen. *Westward Expansion: A History of the American Frontier*. New York: Macmillan, 1982.

De Bruhl, Marshall. *Sword of San Jacinto: A Life of Sam Houston*. New York: Random House, 1993.

Faragher, John Mack. *Daniel Boone: The Life and Legend of an American Pioneer*. New York: Holt, 1992.

Ferris, Robert G., ed. *Explorers and Settlers: Historic Places Commemorating the Early Exploration and Settlement of the United States*. Washington, D.C.: U.S. Department of the Interior, 1968.

Foley, William E., and C. David Rice. *The First Chouteaus: River Barons of Early St. Louis*. Urbana: Univ. of Illinois, 1983.

Ghent, W. J. *The Early Far West: A Narrative Outline, 1540-1850*. New York: Longmans, Green, 1931.

Lamar, Howard R., ed. *The Reader's Encyclopedia of the American West*. New York: Crowell, 1977.

Malone, Dumas, ed. *Dictionary of American Biography*. New York: Scribner's, 1961.

Monaghan, Jay. *Civil War on the Western Border*. Boston: Little, Brown, 1955.

Morgan, Ted. *A Shovel of Stars: The Making of the American West, 1800 to the Present*. New York: Simon & Schuster, 1995.

————. *Wilderness at Dawn: The Settling of the North American Continent*. New York: Simon & Schuster, 1993.

Morison, Samuel Eliot, Henry Steele Commager, and William E. Luechtenburg. *The Growth of the American Republic*, Vol. I. New York: Oxford University Press, 1980.

Murphy, Edmund R. *Henry de Tonty: Fur Trader of the Mississippi*. Baltimore: Johns Hopkins Press, 1941.

Nichols, Alice. *Bleeding Kansas*. New York: Oxford University Press, 1954.

Richardson, Rupert N. *Texas: The Lone Star State*. New York: Prentice-Hall, 1943.

Stiles, T. J., ed. *In Their Own Words: The Colonizers*. New York: Perigee, 1998.

Turner, Francis Marion. *Life of General John Sevier*. Johnson City, Tenn.: Overmountain Press, 1997.

Vestal, Stanley. *The Missouri*. New York: Farrar and Rinehart, 1945.

Weber, David J. *The Spanish Frontier in North America*. New Haven, Conn.: Yale University Press, 1992.

Weems, John E. and Jane. *Dream of Empire: A Human History of the Republic of Texas, 1836-1846*. New York: Simon & Schuster, 1971.

Witman, Arthur. *St. Louis*. Garden City, N.Y.: Doubleday, 1969.

Index

United States, 19, 26, 102, 104; acquisition of Texas by, 11, 105, 124, 132, 135; and Louisiana Purchase, 31, 46, 47, 144, 156; in Mexican War, 110, 135; slavery in, 49, 103, 133, 135, 137-138, 139, 150; in War of 1812, 119; westward expansion of, 2, 7, 9, 29, 53, 71, 88, 96, 99, 119, 122, 138

Walker, Felix, 59

Walker, Thomas, 55, 56

wampum, 22

War of 1812, 29, 49, 91, 119, 122, 123

Washington, D.C., 108-109, 119, 122, 124

Washington, George, 80

Washington County, 80, 81, 85

Washington District, 80

Watauga, Fort, 73-74, 79, 82

Watauga Association, 78, 79, 80

Watauga District, 10-11, 75, 76, 78, 79, 80, 81, 82

Watauga River, 75

Whigs, 152

Whittier, John Greenleaf, 142

Wichita Indians, 156, 157

Wigwam, the, 121, 124

Wilderness Road, 59, 68

Yadkin River, 52

Ysleta. *See* Corpus Christi de Isleta

About the Author

Kieran Doherty is a longtime journalist and business writer as well as a nonfiction writer for young adults. He has written young-adult biographies about William Penn and William Bradford. In the **Shaping America** series, Doherty is the author of *Puritans, Pilgrims, and Merchants: Founders of the Northeastern Colonies*; *Soldiers, Cavaliers, and Planters: Settlers of the Southeastern States*; and *Explorers, Missionaries, and Trappers: Trailblazers of the West*. An avid sailor, he lives in Boynton Beach, Florida, with his wife, Lynne.

Photo Credits